WHAT TO BELIEVE?

WHAT TO BELIEVE?

Twelve Brief Lessons in Radical Theology

JOHN D. CAPUTO

Columbia University Press

New York

Columbia University Press
Publishers Since 1893
New York   Chichester, West Sussex
cup.columbia.edu
Copyright © 2023 Columbia University Press
All rights reserved

Library of Congress Cataloging-in-Publication Data

Names: Caputo, John D., author.
Title: What to believe? : twelve brief lessons in radical theology /
John D. Caputo.
Description: New York : Columbia University Press, [2023] |
Includes bibliographical references and index.
Identifiers: LCCN 2023000870 (print) | LCCN 2023000871
(ebook) | ISBN 9780231210942 (hardback) | ISBN 9780231210959
(trade paperback) | ISBN 9780231558662 (ebook)
Subjects: LCSH: Theism. | Divergent thinking. | Faith. |
Belief and doubt. | Panentheism.
Classification: LCC BD555 .C26 2023 (print) |
LCC BD555 (ebook) | DDC 230—dc23/eng/20230501
LC record available at https://lccn.loc.gov/2023000870
LC ebook record available at https://lccn.loc.gov/2023000871

∞

Columbia University Press books are printed
on permanent and durable acid-free paper.

Printed in the United States of America

*To Nicholas J. Aversa (1932–1993),
known to me as Brother Declan Paul, FSC,
who made all the difference,
and to a band of brothers for our lifelong bond.*

CONTENTS

CONTENTS

ACKNOWLEDGMENTS

MY THANKS to Wendy Lochner and her staff who oversaw the production and publication of this book with dispatch and efficiency, and to the two readers who made several important suggestions for improving it. I also want to thank Joseph Bessler, Marianne Borg, and Robin Meyers—fellow travelers on the path of saving God from religion, as Robin puts it—who gave me invaluable advice and support in the preparation of this book. Finally, I owe more than I can say to a band of brothers, Fr. Robert Albright; John Broderick; Bernard Freiland; Bro. Joseph Mahon, FSC; and Andy Thompson, for their good counsel on this book and for a lifelong friendship. This book grew out of a short article I published— "Panentheism and the Weakening of God," *Modern Believing* 63, no. 2 (2022): 141–47—which explains occassional overlapping phrasings.

THIS IS HOW THE WORLD BEGAN

I CANNOT remember anything older than God, anything in childhood that happened without God, anything older than being Catholic. I cannot remember God without Latin, or Latin without God. Latin was the sacred language, the one spoken to God and by God, or so I thought. Latin, like God, was eternal and omnipresent. As an altar boy I had mastered the faux phonic Latin mimeographed handout—*Ahhd day-um kwi lay-tee-fee-kaht*—that contained the responses to the priest we made at the foot of the altar. We answered for the people who, though perfectly capable of speaking their God-given English, were rendered mute by the Latin. So they followed along in their missals, which had the Latin in the left column, in a Gothic font, which lent it a mysterious, intimidating, otherworldly look, and the English, our earthly language, in the right. Or they quietly said their rosaries, trying to avoid drifting into distraction, whiling away an hour while Latin hummed in the background like the traffic outside the church doors. But it never occurred to any of us to object that anything was out of order. *Ad Deum, qui laetificat juventutem meam*, "to God who gives joy to my youth." Which God did. We were Catholic. Were we ever! Just about everybody I knew was Catholic—the whole world, my whole world. We were not merely *Christian*, a pale, bleached-out word that included Protestants, but Catholic, the one, holy, *catholic*, and apostolic Church, *the* Church, nineteen hundred and fifty years old and counting, an "apostolic succession" that stretched in a straight and unbroken line from St. Peter to southwest Philadelphia!

This is how the world began. Full of candles and incense, black cassocks and white surplices, priests and nuns, Gothic fonts and May processions, a dark picture of *Jesus's Agony in the Garden* in the living room, going to confession on Saturday afternoon and Mass on Sunday morning, in our best clothes, followed by a large midday Italian meal and a lazy afternoon, all the stores being closed. That was the 1940s, the world of pre–Vatican II Catholicism, a spiritual world that, however considerable the changes in the material world around it, had remained unchanged for the last four hundred years. It was as frozen as the Latin language in which it was cast, ever since the Council of Trent (1545–1563) created what we all just called *the Church, Holy Mother, the Church*. I had never heard of Trent. 1545? 1945? What difference does it make? I just thought it was the eternal truth that had dropped from the sky, beginning with the day Jesus ordained Peter as his first pope. If I missed Mass on Sunday, which I never did, I would burn in hell for all eternity. Not a cruel and unusual punishment for a misspent hour on earth, I thought, just getting what I deserved. Missing Mass was a "mortal" sin, which kills the soul, worse than killing the body, which was why they burned heretics back in the day. We did not fear violating the literal "word of God." We feared missing Mass or violating "the teachings of the Church." Either way, a real pope or a paper pope, infallibility or inerrancy, 𝔊𝔬𝔡, in Christian Gothic English, and a fair amount of fear and trembling were fellow travelers.

I have no recollection of ever seriously questioning any of this. In those days, having a question meant that if we asked "the priest" about the teachings of "the Church," we would get "the answer"—all with a definite article—which he himself had learned in the large and intimidating seminary buildings about five miles from our mostly Irish Catholic neighborhood (we Italians were in the minority). I was ready to sign on the dotted line, and I did. I had originally planned to become a priest until I met the De La Salle Christian Brothers, who conducted the Catholic high school I attended in west Philadelphia. The nuns we had in grade school seemed to me celestial creatures, beyond or without gender, supramenstrual beings all covered up with veils that fluttered in the breeze as they made their way back and forth between the convent and the parish school. I found the Brothers engaging, personable, a human face of God. The Brothers called me Jack. The nuns called me John. That said it all. To this day, the difference between *Jack* and *John* for me is the difference between personal familiarity and an impersonal order into which I have been entered by powers beyond my control. The Brothers captured my heart. One Brother in particular, Brother Paul, got me reading things on my own and told me I might be a good writer someday, if only I could correct my grammar (the Philadelphia accent was only improvable, not extinguishable). The nuns were hard-working women, some kind and loving, others a bit fierce, who, however heavenly their vocation, were not above corporeal punishment down here on earth. They ran the schools efficiently while getting pushed around by a patriarchal church. "The Pastor," a tall, gray-haired, and imposing man, who genuinely scared me, settled all disputes. The nuns taught me to listen. The Brothers taught me to speak up. We need both.

I bring all this up so you will understand my beginnings, my point of departure, the point from which I started and also *departed*, as in, I beg to take my leave. This little book is not an autobiography, and it is by no means restricted to Catholics or Christians, rosary-bead-ardent, "recovering," or somewhere in between. "Radical theology" is not confined to religion or even to belief in God; in fact, we might say that *What to Believe?* is a theology for people who *do not* believe in God, for "nones" and other seekers, who are seeking *what they really do believe*, feeling about in the dark for a deeper faith simmering under the swarm of beliefs and disbeliefs swirling overhead. Because religion is making itself increasingly unbelievable, radical theology seeks out what is believable, which makes for a religion without religion, a religion that is not the one you might be expecting. I am telling my story as a case in point, but I could make that point without ever mentioning religion or God. My wager is that others have an analogous story to tell, whatever their beginnings may be. Beginnings are embedded deep in our bowels, our bones, our very being. The end is in the beginning, not as a destiny or deterministic fate, but as a set of possibilities whose outcomes can come as a surprise. Beginnings are like a keyboard on which we are invited to pick out a tune.

So the word *radical* in what follows does not signify a renegade attack, a bitter apostate railing against a cruel childhood— not a bit. Mine was a happily innocent and secure childhood, in a stable family. Sorry, no fearsome father or cold mother to report. I was grateful that I was not born a heretic like my Protestant neighbors (in the minority in our very Catholic blue-collar neighborhood). It was not at all a bad world to grow up in. *Radical* means rethought, restaged, reimagined, reinvented, all in an effort to get at what is *really going on*. So highlight this, it is a maxim to bear in mind: a radicalization is always the radicalization *of* something, something that was passed on to us, transmitted, something already up and running by the time we arrived on the scene, which is pretty much what *tradition* means. The radicalization of a religious tradition means to unearth *what we can really believe* in that tradition even if we no longer believe the official line they were selling us. There are, accordingly, as many radical theologies as there are traditions to radicalize. Radicals are traditionalists, and traditionalists have to be radicals if they want to take the process of transmission seriously, instead of using it as an alibi to cling to the past.

I am by training and inclination a lifelong academic, and I respect scholarly debate. So do not mistake what follows as a breezy twelve-step program in achieving wholeness! This might even leave you in pieces. *But* keep reading; do not let "academic" scare you off. As someone who has spent a lot of time hanging out in academic conference hotel bars, I understand that technical language has its place, but I promise to keep it to a minimum here—to a minimum, but not to zero. Judiciously deployed, it can be quite helpful, which is why I do not hesitate to drop the names of several major philosophers and theologians. These are people with amazing imaginations and highly creative vocabularies, so it will not kill you to be exposed to some of the "big names," which you in turn can drop at happy hour. Just as Carlo Rovelli highlights the most important ideas in contemporary physics while going light on the mathematics, I am trying to simplify without oversimplifying ideas that are too important to be kept under academic lock and key. What follows is neither a trek through a dense scholarly forest nor a visit to *Mister Rogers' Neighborhood*.

I imagine this little book as a daily lesson, six a week (we take the Sabbath off), over the course of two weeks. In the first week, we take up the first half of the argument: to talk you out of thinking of God as a Supreme Being (theism), who I claim does not exist, and to think instead of God as the "ground of being" (panentheism), which is a better bet. In the second week, we take the accent off being (ontology) and stress instead being's worth (axiology), meaning what we love and affirm unconditionally. In so doing we can get at what we will call the *event* that is *really going on in* the name of God. This, I propose, is *what to believe*, what we really can and do believe, regardless of whether or not we "believe in God."

That's the royal road to radical theology, all of which I promise to explain and defend as we go along. So there is a *logical* argument that goes hand in hand with a *historical* development, from theism (classical) to panentheism (modern), and then from panentheism to radical theology (contemporary). Keep an eye on both the story I am telling and the line of thinking I am selling. We do not have any ahistorical thoughts. This history explains how (actually) and why (ideally) theology got radicalized. Radical theology evolved; it was not shot from guns (in more sense than one).

My wager is that what follows will be useful to others who have never so much as met a priest, a nun, or a religious brother. I am sure the view of God I am setting out here would have shocked my parish priests and nuns. It certainly would have shocked young Jack, or John, or Brother Paul, the name I took when I made my "first vows," after the other Brother Paul, who made all the difference in my life and the lives of many others.

FIRST WEEK

Lesson One

GOD DOES NOT EXIST

WE USED the old "Baltimore Catechism," composed in 1885 at the direction of the Third Council of Baltimore, at the time the (all too Irish) Rome of American Catholicism. Maryland was named after the Catholic Queen Mary, wife of King Charles I, who granted a charter to Lord Calvert, the 2nd Lord Baltimore, in 1635. When I entered the Christian Brothers in 1958 after graduating high school, I found myself in the Baltimore District. The first school the Brothers established in the United States was called Calvert Hall, located a block away from the Baltimore Basilica, the first American Catholic cathedral. The Baltimore Catechism was a distillation of the Council of Trent into a compact little Q and A, which the nuns made us memorize and a lot of which I can still recite (the cover was green). The word *catechism* is related to the word *echo*; it literally means to drum something into the ear of someone who can then echo it back. We got to be good at that. Lesson One began:

Q. Who made the world?

A. God made the world.

Q. Who is God?

A. God is the Creator of heaven and earth, and of all things.

Q. What is man?

A. Man is a creature composed of body and soul, and made to the image and likeness of God.

Q. Why did God make you?

A. God made me to know Him, to love Him, and to serve Him in this world, and to be happy with Him forever in the next.

This is a lot of information to get all at once, and it makes quite an impression on a seven-year-old. The implication was, of course (trust me, this was not left in doubt), that I would not be so happy in the next world if I did not get on board in this one. Who was I to argue with all that?

But if I were now asked "Who is God?," safely out of the reach of my priests and nuns, I would say that God—that one, the God a lot of us grew up with, not just Catholics or Christians; the one that is out there in general circulation; the star of stage and screen; the Supreme Being, who sees all, knows all, can do all, who is watching every move we make and is coming to get us if we do not behave ourselves and to whom we turn when things take a turn for the worse—*does not exist*. The most important thing we can say about God is that that God, God, does not exist.

However—keep reading, this is just as important—this does not spell the end of theology, but the beginning of a genuinely *radical* theology. It is not the end of the conversation, but the start of a new one.

I promise you that this is not a doom-and-gloom death-of-God anything-goes nihilism. This is *an* atheism about *the* theism of the Supreme Being under whose constant protection and all-seeing surveillance I, like a lot of others, grew up with, *but* this—cover your ears—is a *theological atheism*. This atheism does theological service as the first step, not the last, on the way to a *post*-theistic *radical* theology or a/theology of what we *really can believe*.

I admit I am trying to be provocative, but this does not mean I am not serious. I am trying to get your attention, trying to get you to bite, on the bet that, if you bite, you will not be sorry. Back in Catholic grade school, this would have landed me in the office of the Mother Superior (on my way out the door). This is not the echo the nuns expected back. So think of this little book as a new revised version of the catechism, a primer in radical theology that never got an imprimatur. The Baltimore Catechism raised great questions for which I have ever since been grateful, like "Who is God?," questions I have been asking myself all my life. It was delivered in daily lessons, which the nuns heard, which I am miming here by serving up twelve brief lessons in radical theology, in an attempt to *save* theology. This is a not a ruse, something passing itself off as theology while secretly trying to undermine it. Radical theology is seriously theological, taking theology seriously. It is an attempt to make contact with something primal, prior to the wars between theism and atheism, religious and secular, prior to 𝕲𝖔𝖉. It is the theology of a kind of protoreligion, an audacious variant of the religion I grew up with, the one with all the candles and clergy.

These pages are addressed to everyone who eventually found 𝕲𝖔𝖉 unbelievable and want to know what, if anything, *is* believable. Demographers tell us that the nones (meaning no religious affiliation) are waxing, and the nuns are waning. But none does not mean nothing, believing *nothing* at all. Nones no longer believe what they were told when they were growing up and now are trying to work out what they *really do* believe. The *really do* is what I mean by *radical* because it is *what is really going on.* (The italics here are flagging what this little book is all about.) The answer to their prayers, to our prayers, to my prayers—and I do believe in prayer (Lesson Four)—I propose, is radical theology, which begins by saying that 𝕯𝖊𝖚𝖘 𝖔𝖒𝖓𝖎𝖕𝖔-𝖙𝖊𝖓𝖘, in Christian Gothic Latin, does not exist but what does exist may surprise you.

But the whole thing does not end there. It is just getting started.

This is not about trashing 𝕲𝖔𝖉. We did well together for a number of years. I was grateful for my "religious vocation." When my children ask me what I was thinking about when I entered the religious life, taking lifelong vows of poverty, chastity, obedience, I smile and say they made me an offer I couldn't refuse. The catechism said to "serve Him in this world, and to be happy with Him forever in the next"—a short temporal life of sacrifice for an eternal life of happiness. That is just good economics. It turned out to be a step along the way of discerning my *real* religious vocation, what I really believe. I never renounced my deeper religious vows to something of elemental import, something deserving of my unconditional faith and allegiance, something *really going on in* the name of the name of God that saturated my youth. Highlight *really going on* every time you come across it: it cuts to the core of what I mean by *radical*, and I will take it up explicitly in Lesson Eight. I say "something," meaning if only I could figure out *what*. He (indulge me for a moment) pursued me down the labyrinthine corridors of my life, and I am forever grateful for that. He—well, let's say, **He**—stretched homogeneously and continuously from God the Father and His Son to the Holy Father (the pope), from his eminence the cardinal archbishop in a big office downtown to our pastor and parish priests, in a long apostolic line of unrelieved masculinity. Jesus said to call only God in heaven your father, but we called a lot of people *Father*. Nowadays we say *She* as much as we can. God is our mother, our father, our friend, our hope, our something. We need all the help we can get. Why tie one hand behind our back?

■ ■ ■

Thinking Radically. What I am calling *radical theology* means nothing more nor less than radical *thinking*. "Dare to think"— that is the motto of the eighteenth-century Enlightenment, which called itself the adulthood, the coming of age, of humankind. I am all for that. The more thinking the better.

But dare to think *radically*, which I think represents an updated Enlightenment, one that is enlightened about the blind spots of the original Enlightenment, on the *double dare* that

(1) if we do *theology* and keep thinking, we will hit *radical* ground. The challenge for theology here is not to be stampeded by the word *radical*, to keep thinking, because theology is a field mined with all kinds of authoritarian conversation-stoppers, like *orthodoxy* and *heresy, inerrant* and *infallible*—where "dare to think" is more like a threat: *just you dare*, and you will rue the day.

(2) If we *think* radically enough, we will eventually hit *theological* ground. The challenge for thinking here is not to be stampeded by the word *theology*. If it is, then thinking ends up with its own kind of dogmatism, the old Enlightenment, which greets religion with a sneer (cultured despising), the old *odium theologiae*, more sophomoric than adult, which I think is as thoughtless in its own way as Bible-thumping is in its way.

I call it a *dare* because it means taking a risk. Radical theology takes the risk of a radical search, being radically "honest to God," to quote the title of Bishop John Robinson's (1919–1983) famous book, which created quite a sensation back in the turbulent 1960s, when I was still a graduate student. In radical thinking the only safe bet is not to play it safe. When I was growing up, I thought that adhering to the "teachings of the Church," orthodoxy, would keep me safe. Orthodoxy was a safe harbor on a stormy sea, where my job was to learn what I was supposed to think (*doxa*, belief), to get it right, to think straight (*orthe*).

But now I think that "orthodoxy" is taking the easy way out. It is like drawing a straight line on a map; it ignores the difficulty of the terrain. I am not waging war on orthodoxy but creating a disturbance *within* it by exposing its contingent and human, all-too-human origins. If we destroy the traditions we inherit, chaos will reign. We begin where we already are, so being radical is always an inflection or modification of something that was up and running without us. We could not be inspired by the prospect of a "radical Jesus" if the memory of Jesus had not been preserved by the texts, traditions, and institutions that have transmitted it. So, if you ask me where I got all this, I could say it is all in the Baltimore Catechism—albeit read in such a way that I would have flunked first grade and been sent to public school with all the Protestants.

Where orthodoxy promises safety, radical theology is risky business. If we take radical theology to heart, then at the end of these lessons we will know less than we think we know. We will discover that "atheism" is vital part of what is going on in the name of God, and "God" is not what they were telling us. We will find that doubt is a vitally important part of faith, and that the name of God is not the answer to a catechism question but a follow-up question put to its answers. A lot of people (pastors among them!) are pretending to believe what they no longer really believe; they are mostly just going through the motions, absent any alternative. Radical theology is the alternative. It proposes something they *really can believe*, which is seriously theological, but it is just not what we have all been told theology was supposed to be. Radical theology does not bring peace; it causes trouble. If you think you have been scammed, you will have to write to the publisher to see if you can get your money back.

Radical does not mean establishing a firm foundation, but contesting something at its roots, risking an unprotected exposure to a more uncertain something or other that we will try to elaborate. We were told that Jesus picked Peter to be the rock-solid foundation upon which he would build his church (Matt. 16:18). But I agree with the scholars who say that is the later Church putting words in his mouth and authorizing *itself*. That is the founder being founded by the followers after the fact. I think Jesus was a more radical figure than that, more a shaker of foundations than a founder, more a prophet and a mystic, and that Jesus would not have known what the later Church was talking about. He was announcing the coming rule of the God of Israel, not of Vatican City. He was talking about God settling the hash of the Romans, not the universal (catholic) rule of Rome, in Latin. That was not his idea; that is was what got him killed. So think of the "radical" as the fiery core beneath the cooled-off encrustation on the surface, beneath—I cannot resist saying it—the "petrification." Or think of radicalization as a desedimentation of aspirations that have settled to the bottom in the tradition, enclosed in the Supreme Being, in the whole history that unfolded in and under the name (of) "God." Radicalization is the re*invent*ion of what I am going to call *the event* (Lesson Eight) harbored in the name of 𝕲𝖓𝖉, in our memory of 𝕲𝖓𝖉, without which these traditions would freeze over, sediment, petrify (Lessons Nine and Ten).

■ ■ ■

Living Radically. If you would like to meet a radical theologian in person, there are two places to look. First, the unemployment line. Relieving the Supreme Being of existence, causing a disturbance among the orthodox, and contributing to the cause of atheism does not play well in most churches—the ones where the orthodox write the paychecks. Theologians who hit radical ground, pastors raising hell (in the name of the kingdom of God, of course) often end up with the want ads for spiritual reading. This sounds facetious, and maybe it is, but there is a serious theological point to be made here. Radical theology is not the theology of a rival church that is trying to build up its membership. It creates a *radical disturbance within* the existing religious bodies.

Let's call that the principle of the *inside/outside*, that the inside is constituted by the exclusion of the outside, because the things the insiders try to keep out are already there on the inside causing a stir, which is why they are trying to keep them out. In radical thinking, if you see a binary opposition, look more closely, and it will break down. See how the one side is inhabited by the other side. Classical theology itself is a bit bipolar, of two minds, not identical with itself. Orthodoxy is inhabited *from within* by heterodoxy, by radical theologians, by the long line of mystics, poets, and radical thinkers who have broken through its sedimented formulas and have broken radical ground, who have from of old been raising hierarchical eyebrows and causing indigestion at the highest levels. These are people listening to the Spirit, not their superiors, and if their superiors listened to them, they would hear more from the Spirit. A lot of the time the people who are really listening to the Spirit do not believe in God at all and are allergic to the word *religion*. Paul Tillich (1889–1965), one of the central figures in radical theology, describes himself as a "border" figure, on the borderline between the inside and the outside. Jacques Derrida (1930–2004), a so-called atheist who worked out the idea of "deconstruction," which is writing philosophy at the "margins," describes a religion *without* religion. If this little book were a novel, they would be the protagonists.

In my own tradition, today's nuns are not your grandparent's nuns. They are among the most outspoken critics of the Church, of the patriarchy, the homophobia, the clericalism, the shocking sexual abuse scandals, the blind and unyielding adherence to the past. If they were given their fair share of the lead, they might be able to stem the mass exodus the Church and the religious orders are experiencing and its steadily falling status among educated people. However, the old boys who have run the Church tell the women that they have it straight from 𝔊𝔬𝔡 that they should be in charge! But take heart. The Apostle Paul himself was quite a radical in his own day and was chased out of many a town—by the orthodoxy of his day. If orthodoxy always wins, the Spirit will expire. It will be impossible to make all things new, to announce good news that actually will be new. Orthodoxy left to itself is the tradition's worst enemy.

The best way to conserve a tradition is not to be a conservative. That is my version of the Catholic principle of tradition, which back in the day would have earned me a one-way ticket to public school.

The other place to find radical theologians is out in the streets, marching on behalf of the cause of social and political justice (nonviolently!). Radical theology is radical thinking, but you only think you are thinking if your thinking is confined to the politesse of seminars and seminaries. When I entered the "religious" life, where we prayed quite a lot, they told me that I had "left the world," meaning "secular" life, where people are too busy making a living to have enough time to pray. Radical theology will have none of that. Still, radical theology is not antimonasticism but a new monasticism, in which the distinction between the religious and secular is contested at its root. Radical theology cuts across and through this distinction by laying bare an elemental and underlying way of thinking and living that undermines and defuses the culture wars this distinction has engendered.

And, increasingly, these culture wars *are* wars, in which, as an old friend of mine said, the religious right say they are protected by the blood of the Lamb, but they still need their guns. God deserves better. God has fallen into the wrong hands. Religion has made itself unbelievable, an enemy of common sense, science, and democratic life, and is well on its way to shaming God out of existence. Radical theology is trying to save God from religion, as Robin Meyers put it so memorably.

I want to be clear that I am not suggesting that anyone who believes in the Supreme Being is a white supremacist or a violent nationalist—God forbid. My point is that the God of classical theology is not identical with itself. It is the best of us and the worst of us, both at the same time. *God* means many different things to many different people, too many things to count or inventory, repeatedly breaking out in loving, expansive, compassionate, generous, selfless, sophisticated, progressive, trailblazing, inspiring people like Dietrich Bonhoeffer and Martin Luther King Jr., or, in the Catholic tradition, Mother Teresa and Dorothy Day, the Berrigan brothers and Thomas Merton, Hans Küng and Pope Francis, including my favorite teachers and oldest friends. The problem is not precisely theism but *doctrinaire* theism, a theism that closes itself off to what is *really going on* in theism, and the same thing goes for doctrinaire atheism or doctrinaire anything. Radical is opposed to doctrinaire as open is to closed, as ecstatic is to static. Happily, we do not have to choose between raging Christian nationalists and sneering rationalists who reduce religion to poison. The one is a gas-filled room, the other a lit match. What I am proposing—a genuinely radical theology—is neither. Without it, I do not think religion has a future, or even deserves to have one, and reason will reduce itself to something less than it really is.

Lesson Two

BRIDGE-BUILDERS AND GROUND-DIGGERS

THE READING *for Today.* If this little book were a sermon, which it is not (mostly, no one is perfect), the text upon which I would have chosen to preach today is the famous scene that Luke stages in Acts 17. I say "stages" because, back in the academy, many New Testament scholars think this episode is all Luke's doing. No matter (we will see why in Lesson Six). Luke has Paul speaking in the Areopagus ("Mars Hill"), where, according to Luke, the philosophers regularly assemble to engage in debates about anything and everything. That part is definitely true. Paul commends the Athenians for the shrines they have built to their many gods, which proves the earnestness with which they seek God, but the one shrine that gets it right is their shrine to the "unknown God." That is one of history's most famous left-handed compliments, for Paul has come to set them straight about the one true God. Apostles tend not to be shrinking violets. The true God is not made by human hands but has himself made everything in heaven and on earth so that anyone anywhere on earth can "search for God and perhaps grope for him and find him—though indeed he is not far from each one of us. For 'In him we live and move and have our being,' as even some of your own poets have said, 'For we too are his offspring'" (Acts 17:24–28).

God is the very element of our life and being. This is to imagine God as not so much "up there," high above us, moving things around and monitoring them from above, like the First Cause on high, but more like the deep ground down below, upon which we rest. If we were all aquatic creatures, God would be the water, not the biggest fish in the sea. Hence, God is—this is important—"not far" from us. That means that to seek God is not to set out in search of a distant entity in a galaxy far, far away, for God is *already here*, within us, all around us, unless we should say that we are within God—which, actually, is even better. The former takes the world's point of view (in the style of philosophy), the latter, God's point of view (in the style of theology). I love them both, equally. God is within us; we are within God.

When I was a member of the De La Salle Brothers, we were instructed to begin each day with a prayer, one we were to repeat each hour: "Let us remember that we are in the holy presence of God." Remember, hourly, that God is "not far." In what follows I want to show we can follow that rule inside or outside religion by *thinking* it through *radically*. So, hang on, here we go.

■ ■ ■

Bridge-Builders and Ground-Diggers. Taking Acts 17 as our text, let us say there are two kinds of theologians. The first, whom I am going to call the *bridge-builders*, think we must build a bridge from the world to God and hope that the world can provide enough support to hold up the bridge. The second, whom I am going to call the *ground-diggers*, think that we do not have to build a bridge because God is the very ground on which we already stand, but that we have to do a little digging (thinking) to see that. The bridge-builders are taking Acts 17 as a construction site while the ground-diggers treat it as an archeological site. The bridge-builders think the ground-diggers are digging themselves into a hole because God is on high. The ground-diggers think the bridge-builders are building a bridge to nowhere, for God is already here; they take themselves to be unearthing hidden treasures, on the bet that, if you dig deep enough, you will hit theological soil. As you might have guessed, we radical theologians have our money on the ground-diggers, and we think the Baltimore Catechism was written by bridge-builders (who were following the instructions of the *pontifex maximus*).

If you are up on these matters, you can probably hear me paraphrasing Paul Tillich on the "two types of philosophy of religion." Tillich is my favorite official theologian. I have several favorite *un*official ones, some of whom are officially "atheists." (Remember, if you deprived me of the word *God* I would still keep talking.) Tillich thought Thomas Aquinas (1225–1274), the intellectual hero of the Catholic world in which I grew up, was a bridge-builder, and that Augustine (354–430), historically the inspiring spirit of Protestantism, was a ground-digger. Aquinas constructed five proofs to bridge the gap from the world to God (*but* Aquinas also thought that

God was immanent in the world precisely in virtue of his transcendent power). Augustine stayed home and found God within himself in the *Confessions* (*but* he also thought that God was transcendent, that by going *in* he was also going *up*). (So this is complicated.)

Tillich follows Augustine, and we radical theologians follow Tillich. If we have to "find God," and we do, that is not because God is an "alien being" (𝔊𝔫𝔡 = a Supreme Being transcending space and time), but because we are *alienated from God* and do not realize that God is that in which we *already* live and move and have our being. The bridge-builders think we have to find some way to attain the truth. The ground-diggers think we are already *in* the truth, that God is truth, and that the task is to *unearth* its truth.

So the "method" of both philosophy and theology (in radical theology that very distinction is a ladder we will climb and then kick away, in Lesson Eleven) is Augustinian, which is to recover what was never lost, to acquire what we already possess, to remember what we already know, to become who we already are. *Noli foras ire*, Augustine said. Do not go out and about looking for God. God is not far. God is right here—God-within-us or we-within God—waiting to be found.

■ ■ ■

The Unconditional Is More Primordial than God. Here is where you have to bear with me and not be scared off by a bit of academic language. To sort this out, Tillich says that *God is unconditional, but the unconditional is not God.* That is an enigma in need of an explanation, and there is one. The unconditional is the condition of everything *else*, but nothing is the condition of *it*. It is that than which we *cannot think* (epistemology), and we *cannot want* (axiology), and there *cannot be* (ontology) anything *prior*. So, the next question is, where is the unconditional to be found? Tillich's answer is that *God* is unconditional, which is how God is God, *but* the unconditional itself cannot be identified with or restricted to God. Why not? Because the unconditional is always and everywhere and cannot be shut up inside a word or a being, not even a Supreme one. Furthermore, while the unconditional is an office that has traditionally been held by God, there are other candidates for the job. God could in principle (ever since the Enlightenment) be voted out of office. A "materialist" thinks this office should be held by "matter," and nowadays the AI people think it should go to "information."

According to Friedrich Schelling (1775–1854)—not a household name but a great nineteenth-century German philosopher who was Tillich's muse and inspiration—the unconditional is the *prius*, meaning what is absolutely prior, more primordial than God, prior to anything we would say about it, which would always arrive too late (*posterius*). This led Schelling to describe the unconditional as *das Unvordenkliche* (literally, the absolutely un-pre-thinkable). I promise not to bury you in German philosophical jargon, but this is one of those words that philosophers come up with that I really love, and that I will come back to as we proceed. The unconditional is what gets there prior to thought, what is already up and running by the time thought arrives on the scene, before thought can lay down the *conditions* under which existing things would be possible.

This represented a rebuke to the Enlightenment philosophers like Immanuel Kant (1724–1804), who described "pure reason" as the faculty of laying down in advance, a priori, the conditions under which experience is possible. But Schelling said thought came a posteriori. Kant treated "Reason"—I capitalize it here to show it the respect Kant had for it—as the Supreme Court that makes the final call as to whether things have the right to exist, whether there is a "sufficient reason" for them to be. So even God had to appear before the Court and make His [sic] case, divine hat (or crown) in hand. Schelling thought the opposite. He said that the unconditional precedes any conditions reason would set, any demands reason would make, any distinction thinking would draw, even the distinction between the thinking self or subject and the very object of thought. However proudly, loudly, and authoritatively Reason dictates the conditions under which things may be, the unconditional is not intimidated. If Reason says, that cannot be, being replies, and yet here we are.

■ ■ ■

How Can We Speak of the Unconditional? This creates an obvious problem. If the unconditional is prior to thought itself, how is it possible to think of it or to say anything about it? After all, anything we would ever think or say about the unconditional would be conditioned—that is, drawn from our language, our culture, our experiences, which are always concrete, particular. The unconditional is always and everywhere, but anything we would say about it would be datable and locatable. As the famous

German poet who used the pen name of Novalis (1772–1801) said—this was also a German pun—we seek the unconditional (*das Unbedingte*), but everywhere we turn we run into conditions (*Dinge*).

However, this does not mean we cannot say anything *at all* about the unconditional. It means we cannot say anything about it that is not *mediated* by conditions. When it comes to the unconditional, we have to use mediators, intermediaries. But then we have to constantly bear in mind the distinction between the mediat*or* and what is being mediat*ed*, and not confuse one with the other, which is a bigger problem than you might think.

The difficulty we face here is that nobody has ever directly met or experienced the "unconditional" and for a very good reason. The unconditional is not a *particular thing we could ever meet*. We cannot be immediately united with the unconditional—what the mystics of old sought—because there is no "thing" there to unite with, to wrap your arms around. The unconditional is the underlying source or support of the things we do meet, their background or element or presupposition or condition. It is the forest, not the trees. There was a cartoon in the *New Yorker* some years ago in which an older fish greets two young fish by asking them, "How's the water, boys?" After the old fish has passed by, the one young fish asks the other, "What the hell is water?" To offer a more sophisticated if daring comparison, we might say that the unconditional is like a "field" in contemporary physics, where a "thing" is an excitation of the field.

The unconditional is only found *in* things, and things come to be as mediations or expressions *of* the unconditional. They are distinct but never found separately, like up and down. They belong together in a circle of mutual implication: the unconditional is *recessed in* things, and things gain us *access to* the unconditional. So, speaking of the unconditional is not impossible, but we have to be careful, first, because we may confuse the one for the other, which in theology is called idolatry, and second, because what is mediated requires regular remediation (updating, reforming, transforming).

■ ■ ■

Only a Symbol. The next step is this. If we say in theology that *God* is the unconditional, then we are saying "God" is a *symbol*, a figure, in which the unconditional is mediated, imaginatively constructed. Unprethinkability does not mean we cannot think about the unconditional, but that our thinking of it will always take place in *symbols* that *mediate* it to us. Then the task will be not to find a way get beyond the symbols—for that would leave us bereft of any access at all—but to come up with symbols *worthy* of the unconditional and to avoid unworthy ones. So, if someone proposes that the unconditional means doing whatever is necessary to get rich and powerful, that is telling us more about them than the unconditional.

That means that symbols are important, that they are to be taken seriously. They are not arbitrary contrivances that somebody made up. They have paid their own way, having been forged in the fires of history. They have earned respect, earned their place as concrete, sensuous, and inspiring ways we give words and images to matters that, as Tillich says, are a "matter

of ultimate concern," a formula upon which it would be difficult to improve when it comes to saying what we mean (in
Christian Latin English) by *religion*. (I also like this definition
because it makes no mention of clergy, excommunications, candles, or collection plates.) Far from being fanciful fictions,
symbols have to do with being "seized by" something primordial, something prior to us, something that, Tillich says, is not
a *particular being* but represents the very power of *being-itself*.
Talking about "being-itself" is called *ontology*—literally, being-
talk, just like *theology* is literally God-talk.

Still, if the truth be told, is *symbol* not just a fancy way of
admitting that religion, God and theology are purely subjective, nothing more than anthropomorphic projections, human
fancies and human features being attributed to something else?
That theory is as old as Xenophanes (d. 475 BCE), but it was
famously put forward in the nineteenth century by Ludwig
Feuerbach (1804–1872), who thought that theology is ultimately
(radically) anthropology, where we human beings project our
own qualities onto an alien being called God. The work of
philosophy for Feuerbach is "criticism"—that is, to rewind theology, to run it in reverse and return these divine predicates to
us, which is where they came from in the first place.

In radical theology, Feuerbach is not so much wrong as only
half right. We certainly do project, but we are projecting something by which we have been previously injected. We use the
power of our imagination to construct images, analogies, simi-
les, symbols, metaphors, and personifications, to tell stories, to
compose song and dance—*but* (as you can tell by now, *but* is a
really big word in radical theology) all this comes in *response* to

something *prior* to us, something primordial, more elemental, by which we have been seized, something that has us before we have it. Remember, the unconditional is the prius, the prior, the a priori. Of course we project. We compose dance and songs, but our songs are less of our own composition than they are the music the world is playing on us. The world supplies the music, for which we supply the words. Projection is the projection of the *other in me*, by which I have been previously taken hold.

To see *what is really going on*—remember to highlight this expression—in symbols, Tillich says, there are two things to keep in mind. First, if you truly understand what a symbol is, you will never say, "It is *only* a symbol." Symbols go all the way down, into the bowels of being-itself, into our own bowels. They are visceral; they cut deep, sometimes literally. People kill and get killed over symbols. Cynical people try to harness the great power of the symbol of "God" to serve their own political purposes. Think of the violence that can break out over the treatment of the national flag. Second, never confuse a symbol with what it is a symbol *of*, which is the unconditional; never confuse God with religion or a book or an institution.

In symbols, we are making contact with the depths, with the ground of being. They are not terms of art in an academic debate. Symbols have been fashioned by the blood, sweat, and tears of a historical community, and they cannot be arbitrarily created or discarded. When they break down it is not because they have been "refuted" by a logical argument back in the faculty lounge. They have died away in the streets, lost their power to give word and image to our bonds with being, and the community can no longer recognize itself in them. Then they cannot be defended by a logical argument. So, the idea is not to get beyond symbols, but to nourish symbols *worthy* of the unconditional.

To summarize, our preferred method of dealing with the unconditional, of getting at what is really going on, is ground-digging, unearthing the underlying condition, ground, source, field, support, horizon, element or presupposition—not bridge-building, setting out in search of Somebody off in the Seventh Heaven. We are always and already in contact with the unconditional, not because we have managed to establish contact with it, but because it contacted us before we had anything to say about it. That contact is not something we do; it is what we *are*, so if we discover the unconditional we will also discover ourselves. If that contact were broken, we would vanish in that very instant; that would be the end of us. The task is to have the ears to hear and the eyes to see "that in which we live and move and have our being." That is radical theology.

■ ■ ■

God. This line of thinking about the unconditional has huge implications for theology, for how we are to think and speak (*logos*) of God (*theos*)—and how *not* to speak of God. It represents a sea change, a seismic shift. It is like Einstein rewriting the physics books in 1905. It would have been very shocking to me back when I was growing up in "the Church," and even today I feel a little chill down my spine whenever I read this famous text in Tillich:

God is no object for us as subjects. He [*sic*—it was 1946] is always that which precedes this division [the prius]. But, on the other hand, we speak about him and we act upon him, and we cannot avoid it, because everything which becomes real to us enters the subject-object correlation. Out of this paradoxical situation the half-blasphemous and mythological concept of the "existence of God" has arisen. And so have the abortive attempts to prove the existence of this "object." To such a concept and to such attempts, atheism is the right religious and theological reply.

Everything we have been talking about so far is at work in this famous passage, and everything hereafter will flow from it. Here is the *first step* on the royal road to radical theology, the first stage of divesting 𝕲𝖔𝖉 of his fearful Gothic eminence, the first major move in the mobilization of radical theology: *from the Supreme Being to being-itself,* from the biggest fish in the sea to the sea itself. If it were up to me, this passage would be framed and hung in the main entrance of every school of theology and seminary, and, if I were not against this sort of thing—this is what the fiercest of our nuns did to us—I would make all the seminarians memorize it on their first day under threat of corporeal punishment.

Tillich's language is strong but precise.

On the *one hand*, when we speak of God it is *unavoidable* that we would think of a particular of object of thought, a particular being. That is a demand of common sense and of our imagination and indeed of thought itself—to every act of thinking (the subject) there corresponds an object of thought. What could be more obvious? That goes for the unconditional—if we try to think of it, we unavoidably think of some thing or object. How could we not? But there is more. Because in religion the unconditional goes under the name of God, that means—and this is a point that cannot be overemphasized—this is also a demand of *piety*. When we *pray*, we pray to *Someone*, to God as to another person, another being, albeit a Supreme Being, with all the omni attributes imaginable, which feminist theologians call with a wink the Big Guy in the Sky. I will come back to this point about prayer in Lesson Four because it is very important. Without prayer, without an idea of what is going on in prayer, we are howling at the moon if we are talking about religion.

On the *other hand*, the right response to *this* God—God, God as an object, as a particular being, however Supreme, whose existence is open to proof and disproof—is *atheism*! Of course, Tillich is a theologian, and he cashed his paychecks from a "theological seminary." So this is a religious and theological atheism, just as I promised in Lesson One. Why *half-blasphemous*? Because it contracts the infinite expanse of being-itself to a distinct being, however supreme; it confuses the infinite and the finite, the unconditional and the conditional. Once the very question of the *existence* of that being is *on the table*, and we can argue about it, being-itself—that in which we live and move and have our being—has fled the scene; the umbilical cord of theology has been cut. It would be like the two young fish arguing about the existence of water. All that remains would be the bridge-builders trying to build an expanse that can cross from the finite to the infinite, which is never going to happen.

Why *mythological*? Because it *personifies* the ground of being, treating it as if it were "somebody," the way the natural religions personify thunder and lightning, or like St. Francis's canticle to Brother Sun and Sister Moon. Personifying is not bad, mind you, not in itself, not by a long stretch. Personifying is mythological, but it is a myth to think that mythology is not important. Mythology is not bad, unless we *forget* that it is a personification, a mythological act. In premodern times, myths were lived in, innocently, but in postmodern times, myths are "broken" (Tillich)—that is, we know they are myths, but we still treasure them and do not simply dismiss them disdainfully as they did in modern times (the old Enlightenment).

Joining *both hands* together (as if in prayer), Tillich is saying that the name of God is a *symbol* of the unconditional, and remember the rule: symbols are important—without them, we will have no access, no way to speak of the unconditional—*but* do not confuse the symbol with what it is a symbol *of.* When you fall into that confusion in religion, the result is blasphemy. That is why Tillich's language is so strong ("half-blasphemous," "mythological," "atheism"—strong, but precise). So *this* atheism is not the end of theology but the beginning of a *new* theology, a deeper *post*-theistic theology. *This atheism is a theological critique of theology*; it represents a theology of "theism transcended," the *first step* in establishing a *radical* theology.

■ ■ ■

The Mystical. Actually, going back to the bipolarity of theology, the principle of the inside/outside—that you can always find

the stirrings of the outside on the inside, that the inside is constituted by attempting to exclude the outside—atheism has
regularly played a role *within* theology. We have heard something like this atheism before from the mystics, well-known
radicals incurring the wrath of orthodoxy. Meister Eckhart
(1260–1327), who is my favorite mystic, my mystic of choice,
advanced a kind of mystical atheism when he prayed God to
free him of 𝕲𝖔𝖉, which is to condense radical theology into a
formula that also cannot be improved upon. Here is a prayer to
the God beyond 𝕲𝖔𝖉, to which there corresponds a radical theology of what is *really going on* with God. The mystics are
always far ahead of the rest of us, and they are not to be confused with the self-lacerations or visions of preternatural
beings that you find in the "lives of the saints." They made us
read those books when I was in the novitiate, and I hated them.
I did not take religious vows in order to disavow my mind. I
did not sign up for allowing nonsense like that to get inside
my head. When the bell tolled the hour for the "spiritual reading" on our schedule, I discreetly reached for Frank Sheed's
Theology and Sanity, which I covered in brown paper, as my
antidote to the lives of the saints, which seemed like theology
and insanity.

But even here we must advance with care. When Tillich
himself speaks of "God beyond God," he does not mean the
God of *classical* Christian mysticism *transcending space and time*,
but the opposite, an *awareness* of a ground of being deeply
embedded *in space and time*. "Beyond" does not mean up but
down; it does not mean higher but deeper; it does not mean far-
ther but closer. He moves beyond the alien God to the God

who is nearer to us than we are to ourselves, beyond any particular being to its "ground," which is being-itself. So, while there is a mystical sense of life in Tillich to which I will return (Lesson Five), he means an awareness of and attention to the ground of being, nothing Neoplatonic, which is unbiblical. Tillich does not mean becoming one with the eternal One, nor does he embrace a pure intuition of the One accompanied by a disdain for reason. That is precisely the *unmediated* unity with the unconditional he rejects, the desire for which has landed classical theology in a ditch.

The many people leading generous and compassionate lives religion produces is an important point in radical theology, where religion is a form of life *in* time, not outside it. Religion is not a rehearsal (emphasis on hearse) for death, resting in eternal peace, *requiescat in pace*, RIP. When we become one with the One, the only thing left to do is call the undertaker. Radical theologians prefer to remain as long as possible among the many, to become multitudes, as Walt Whitman said, to remain many with the many. Or, as Woody Allen said, I do not want to live on in my works or live on in my children; I want to live on in my apartment. Radical theology is not an exercise in Neoplatonic escapism but an *escape from* Neoplatonism, the undoing of the damage Neoplatonism has done to the New Testament. Neoplatonic dualism is one of the main reasons religion has made itself so unbelievable. Radical theology is the antidote to Neoplatonism; it sets out in search of what is believable, right here in space and time. For Tillich, "eternal life" is a *symbol*. Of what? Of keeping centered on the ground of being, being of steady purpose in the shifting tides of time and circumstance, a symbol of a kind of spiritual gyroscope that keeps us from tipping over, always feeling about for the presence of God *in* space and time. The mystical element in Tillich means a way of getting in touch with the depth of the things all around us, not attaining their height; it means living life without succumbing to the noise and dissipation of life—and he did not have to deal with the social media of today—and sustaining an awareness of that in which we live and move and have our being.

■ ■ ■

Theopoetics. This point about symbols also shows that theology is not in any *strong* sense theo*logy*. All the discursive delicacy we have been exercising, all the tiptoeing around finding a way to speak of the unconditional when we are everywhere surrounded by conditional things, all this means that, when push comes to shove, theo*logy* must become theo*poetics*. Talking about God does not come down to concepts, propositions, and arguments (the only remedies in their medical bag when the doctors of philosophy arrive on the scene). Talking about God ultimately comes down to other discursive resources—images and figures, metaphors and metonyms, symbols and allegories, parables and paradoxes, stories and striking sayings, songs and dance—in which we seek to express the grip the unconditional has upon us, by which we have been seized from a time out of mind. Notice that whenever Jesus talks about God, he ends up telling a story about mustard seeds, treasures hidden in a field, wedding feasts, and the like. Jesus was a great theopoet, and the kingdom of God was his poem (in "Christianity" he became the poem). Radical theology is theopoetics, and theopoetics is "weak" theology, meaning that it weakens the conceptual grip *we* think we have on being-itself and fesses up to the prior grip it has on *us*, switching us from the nominative *we* to the accusative *us*.

I hasten to add that theopoetics is not flowers on the altar. It does *not* mean a poetry that supplies the *ornamentation* of an already conceived theology. It is not a poetic flourish that decorates an already constituted system of theology or something that adorns a finished theology. Theopoetics is instead an exercise of *creative imagination*, one that is constantly imagining the unconditional, envisioning things otherwise, attempting to forge ahead down unbeaten paths, to produce something new, to think what has never been and maybe never will be, the first, last, and only recourse when thinking has run up against the unprethinkable.

Lesson Three

THAT'S PANTHEISM, THAT'S HORRIBLE!

PANTHEISM. I remember growing up thinking that pantheism—what I thought was pantheism—was just crazy. Everything is God. The world is God. How could anyone believe that? Pantheism seemed to me as good as atheism, or, rather, as bad, because it denies the opening line of the Baltimore Catechism: God is not the world. God is a Supreme Being who *created* the world! How hard is that to understand?

So it seems that reading Tillich has made me crazy. Is not Tillich's post-theism, his theological atheism about theism, really just another name for *pantheism*? And is not pantheism just atheism by another name? That is a curious point. One term says all is God, the other that nothing is. Why would we ever confuse them? Read the catechism! Blame the bridge-builders, the theists, for whom pantheism *is* atheism. Why? Because, either way, there is no 𝔊𝔬𝔡, no distinct Supreme Being up there. Pantheism, they complain, leaves us trapped in the world, with no way out, no exit, no transcendence. That's horrible! In fact, for the theists, pantheism is *worse*, because at least atheists are honest—no more God—but pantheism is a scam, trying to speak of God just when it does not believe there is one.

If we ask Tillich if this is pantheism, his answer would be, if you like—just so we understand pantheism *properly*. There's the rub. *Atheism* is a relative term, depending on what you mean by *theos*. Because the early Christians were not polytheists, the Romans called them *atheists*. When Socrates denied that the sun and the moon were gods, the Greeks called him an atheist. Understanding pantheism properly means bearing in mind Lesson Two, that the unconditional is not *immediately identical* with conditioned things but *mediated* by them, and conversely, that conditional things are not immediately identical with the unconditional but are ways of *mediating* it. When theists use the word as a term of abuse, a stick with which to beat their opposition, they understand it in a completely ham-fisted way, mockingly, *without the mediation*. Pantheism does not mean that the broken lawn mower in the garage is God, or that boozy old Uncle Harry is God. It means that things have a depth dimension, that they express the power of being, which is divine, that everything (*pan*) does, all creatures great and small, just so long as we are *paying attention*, and for the religious sensibility it is that depth dimension which is divine (*theios*).

Nobody ever explained that to me back in the day, but it explains a lot of things. It explains why contemporary physicists are constantly losing their breath at the things they are discovering—as *scientists*. Right now, for example, millions of infinitesimal particles called *neutrinos* are passing through our body, having traveled here from a time and place out of mind at the other end of the universe. As we find when we read people like Stephen Hawking, Carl Sagan, Brian Greene, Sean Carroll, or Carlo Rovelli, it does not take long before physicists who do not "believe in God" begin musing over the "mystery" of the cosmos, as in *mysterium tremendum et fascinans*, the famous description of the mystery we call God proposed by Rudolf Otto (1869–1937). That does not mean that radical theology is rocket science, but it does mean that rocket science is theological.

Suppose that Uncle Harry was your much-loved favorite uncle, a source of boundless joy in your childhood, and that one day, quite by accident, you come upon his old hat, a fondly held family keepsake of this dear man, now long dead. The hat, a shabby old thing, opens up the whole world of your childhood, an ocean of memories come flooding in—your parents, your cousins, the laughter that flowed freely in your childhood home, holiday dinners, and, yes, life and death. Even the simplest thing—for Marcel Proust it was a cup of tea and a madeleine—can be the occasion of an encounter with the *depth* of things, of youth and time, of being-rather-not, of being-itself, a whole world of love, and "God is love." That is radical theology in action. It is also the philosophical foundation of Romanticism and of Samuel Taylor Coleridge's (1772–1834) interest in Schelling, of the poet finding God in a sunflower or a grain of sand (Lesson Five).

The *pan* in *pantheism* shows up in the way *anything* can be magic. Anything you like, however humble, the humbler the better, can be the occasion of a microtheology. Take a beat-up hat, an old pair of shoes, a broken tree branch, and a painter can light it up. Instead of making a copy of reality (the mimetic theory of art), the painter magnifies its reality, intensifies its being, puts a frame around things and makes them a window through which we catch sight of—what? Tillich would say the ground of being, which is what his reverence calls *God* on Sunday morning just before he passes around the ecclesiastical hat. Poets do the same thing with the most commonplace words, and musicians can do it with commonplace sounds.

But the point is that you do not have to be Einstein or Coleridge, Schelling or Shelley, to appreciate all of this. All you need is to be *alive* and to be *aware*, to be *paying attention* to *what is going on* in the most commonplace things in life, all of which stir with depth, which is the sum and the substance of pantheism and the heart of what the word *mystical* means if we do not mystify it. Pantheism is not horrible; it is just paying attention, which in the Scriptures is called having the eyes to see and the ears to hear. In philosophy, it is called *hermeneutics*, which is defined as the *subtilitas explicandi*, having the right touch, the light touch (*subtilitas*) to unfold, lay out (*explicandi*) what lies beneath the surface, or the *subtilitas intelligendi*, the delicate ability to read between the lines (*inter* + *legere*), approaching things insightfully, with understanding, discernment, attention. Try listening to the music the ocean makes at midnight. (Tillich had a vacation home on the Long Island coast!) Then ask yourself, what is going on?

If the ground of being is what Tillich means by God, and if making contact with the ground of being is what he means by

religion, then religion can be found *anywhere*—just as Paul said
to the Athenians—in a sunflower or a soup kitchen, in science
or a work of art, or even in an old hat. That, I am proposing, is
a pantheism that makes sense, which is not crazy, and it is also
a religion in which *we can actually believe*, as opposed to the religion that is making God unbelievable, into God's own worst
enemy. Religion radically conceived can be believed by anyone
with a heart, anyone who is paying attention. The unconditional is able to be found always and everywhere, so accessing
it is not a regional affair. That means it is not a thing we do in
houses of worship on the Sabbath ("religious"), as opposed to
what we do in business offices the rest of the week ("secular").
Religion in this sense is not a *particular part* of the culture,
Tillich said; it is the *depth dimension* in *any part* of the culture
you choose. So, *wherever* you find yourself located in the culture, *start digging*, and if you *dig deep enough* you will hit a religious core. Every culture has a theology (and nowadays usually
more than one), otherwise it is just a place where people hang
their hat, and every theology requires a culture, otherwise it is
just words sitting on dusty bookshelves (or thumb drives, or,
nowadays, on the cloud).

The language of pantheism makes the traditionalists ner-
vous, but, once again, according to the principle of the inside/
outside, the *experience* it is describing is found there, right in
the heart of the tradition, in theologians (Eriugena, St. Francis, Joachim of Fiore, and Nicholas of Cusa), poets, visionaries,
and mystics from of old. The question is, what we are to make
of it? Does the world *embody* God (pantheism) or does it *image*
God (theism)? Is it the body of God or just made in the

likeness of God? One unnerving question pantheism raises is, if all this is so, then why exactly do we need to have religion in the *narrow* or *traditional* sense? Why pay for the upkeep on houses of worship? And then, heaven help us, how will his reverence earn a decent living?

Before we go too far in this direction—and, I admit, I am tempted—we should recall that *radical* does not mean to plant an explosive and blow things up. *Radical* means the radicalization of *something* of which radical thinkers say there is a depth dimension. Radical theology is not the theology of a separate and competing religion for which I am going to start soliciting donations. Just as the ground of being does not add one more being to the count, just so radical theology is not adding one more religion to the count. Radical theology is probing the depth dimension *in* the religions we already have, and God knows we already have enough of them.

So in radical theology we do not say there is no need for religion in the narrow sense. We just say that (1) the traditional religions do not hold the patent on the unconditional; they are *not the only place* we can make contact with the depth in things, as the bridge-builders try to make us think; and (2) they are bipolar, of two minds, *disturbed from within*, because they contain something (an excess, a recess, the unconditional) that they cannot contain (keep to themselves), and to the extent they fess up to that, everyone is better off, including them. That is the inside/outside principle. Radical theology is stirring within religion in the conventional sense, stirring it up, making trouble there, salutary trouble. The problem is that the powers that be, the hierarchy, are often too ready to show it the door, unless, as also happens, the pastor or the bishop is the radical trouble-maker, and the aging congregation shows him the door.

We can start radical theology anywhere. Begin where you are and start digging. That is why I began these lessons by stating where I began, in the world of pre–Vatican II Catholicism. The traditional religious bodies remain, if not the only, at least a *good place* to *start*. It is no accident that my favorite account of radical theology, of a religion of the depth of things, is to be found in a "professional" theologian like Tillich! It makes perfect sense to *start* with religion in the narrow sense because there we find centuries of texts, teachers, and traditions turning on the name (of) "God," deep meditations on "God" as a resonant symbol of the *unconditional*, a surpassingly deep and provocative word, not just a clever term of art somebody coined in a scholarly journal.

But, as these very same scriptures say, there are no temples—no religion in the narrow sense—in the heavenly Jerusalem (Rev. 21:22) because there God is all in all. That means that what we call *religion*, as a particular part of the culture, commanding our attendance on the Sabbath, which we distinguish from the *secular*, which means what we do the rest of the week, all that is Plan B. This regionalization of religion—which is, by the way, more of a "modern" development; in premodern times, not so much—is testimony to our alienation from God, who is not an alien being, bearing witness to our inattentiveness. If everyone were paying attention, and not distracted by the noisy surfaces of the world, it is his reverence who would be reading the "want ads."

■ ■ ■

Panentheism. So is radical theology pantheism? I agree with Tillich: if you like. If you keep in mind the logic of mediation, that pantheism means not that each and everything *is* God, but that God is *in* all and all are *in* God, that individual things come to be and pass away, but the underlying ground of being endures forever. Then would it not be clearer and less confusing to speak of pan*en*theism, a word which puts the stress on the *being-in*, God-*in*-all, all-*in*-God? If you like. "What I dislike," Tillich said, "is the easy way in which these phrases are used: theism is so wonderful and pantheism so horrible. This makes the understanding of the whole history of theology impossible." This is a very important point. Classical theists are like the rest of us; they try to make what they like sound good and what they don't like sound horrible. "Atheism" for a lot of them—not Hans Küng (1928–2021) and other progressive theologians—is horrible and heartless, cold, cruel, and cowardly (not to be found in foxholes), while, for a ground-digger like Tillich, atheism (properly understood, with a little subtilitas) is the right religious and theological response to theism. So, Tillich concludes, "if you call it panentheism, that would be all right, because that means everything is in God."

As usual, the words we use depend on how we are using them. Even so, I myself think that *panentheism* is the superior choice of words, less misleading, a time-saver, because we then do not have to spend so much time explaining what we do *not* mean. But, like Tillich, the radical theologian in me hates to give up the word *pantheism*, just because a lot of theists think it is so horrible. Imagine the reaction had I announced to my nuns in my back to school essay that I had used the summer vacation to become a pantheist! That is what Mary-Jane Rubenstein calls the "*pan*ic" at "*pan*theism." Versions of panentheism have long been a lure for many classical theologians, who have an inner sympathy for it, but the word *pantheism* throws a lot of others into a panic. I consider that a constructive panic if it serves to loosen the grip of a too-tight "theism," which is the first step in radicalizing theology.

So pantheism plays a *strategic* role in twisting free of theism, even if, back in the faculty lounge, panentheism is probably the more precise term. Given how much time theists have spent trying to scare the daylights out of the rest of us with their 𝔊𝔬𝔡, panentheists are just demanding equal time. What's fair is fair. Like many great classical theologians, we cut a wide swath around a 𝔊𝔬𝔡 who makes space and time look like a vale of tears, a time of trial, in exchange for which—if we can just keep all the rules and behave ourselves—we will be rewarded with a heavenly banquet (just when we and our taste buds will all be good and dead). That line has taken the joy out a lot of lives. For us, in radical theology, the theism those theists are selling is snake oil, and pantheism, which is panning that theism, is causing them to panic.

A bit of schadenfreude, I admit.

Lesson Four

DO RADICAL THEOLOGIANS PRAY?

IN MY experience, the thing that most maddens a lot of theists is that, whatever we call it, *pantheism* or *panentheism*, *theopoetics* or *radical theology*, they suspect the whole thing is a ploy, something passing itself off as religion just where there is none. Their proof is simple: without a Supreme Being, there is no one to whom we can pray, and, if there is no prayer, there is no religion in any serious sense, just the show, just the semblance. Do radical theologians pray, or is their talk about religion just talk? If they really pray, to *whom* would they pray, and from whom do they expect an answer to their prayer?

Radical theology, they complain, is strictly an academic undertaking, something to write about in the journals, a way to get academic promotion and tenure, but of no interest to real people in the pews, who actually pray. As one who has spent a lot of time in the pews and on my knees—back in the day, I actually had calluses on my knees—I take this complaint seriously. The lesson for today is to see whether and how there is prayer, *personal prayer*, in radical theology, taking the personal first, then the prayer.

■ ■ ■

Persons. The "strategic" role, getting in the face of something, played by pantheism, is what Jacques Derrida—my favorite unofficial theologian, who says he "rightly passes for an atheist"—calls "reversal." For example, we noticed earlier that Tillich himself habitually referred to God in the masculine—even though the ground of being is not a male. Indeed, if we were forced to assign it a gender, it suggests something more like a womb, like Mother Earth, or "the face of the deep," as Catherine Keller has so beautifully expounded. It suggests a great uterine sea from which living things emerge, not a Big Guy in the Sky creating things with the blink of an eye, or with a mere whisper of His Imperial Word. So let it be written, so let it be done—or else! Furthermore, there are plenty of feminine images of God in the scriptures (like the *Shekinah*, Wisdom, the Spirit).

Sophisticated theists like Thomas Aquinas, whom I studied "religiously" as a young student brother and Catholic philosopher, have always known very well that, as a pure spirit, the Supreme Being does not have genitalia and transcends sexual difference. When the tradition, including Jesus, speaks of God in the masculine, as "our Father," Aquinas said that is "analogical" language. That's progress. *But* the problem is that this was considered a *better analogy* than "our Mother." That reflects an ancient prejudice, shared by Greeks and Jews, and very congenial to theism, that the masculine principle is active and form giving and the feminine principle is passive and form receiving, *mater* merely meaning the *materia* in which the seed grows.

I say *congenial*, not *congenital*, because we are hardly lacking in theologians today who are theists who criticize it, but it is certainly congenital to the Christians who think big strong (white) men should run everything—the family and the parish, the country and the cosmos, and who want to take the kingdom of God with real violence. Metaphors matter. When it comes to the unconditional, they are all we have to go on. So, when feminist theologians retaliate and retranslate the Bible by referring to God as her and speak of "She Who Is," as in Elizabeth Johnson's groundbreaking book, they are *reversing* an odious tendency, giving as good as they get, getting in the face of patriarchy, just the way pantheism gets in the face of theism, giving patriarchy its comeuppance. Good for them!

To this we must add that, as important as it is, reversal is not final. Reversal is meant eventually to lead to "displacement," at which point we realize that, since God does not have genitalia, both masculine and feminine are historical constructions, both equally valid symbols, neither of which is literal, nor is there any need to choose between them. Both are valuable constructions but both are in need of *deconstruction*, the word Jacques Derrida made famous, which returned the favor and made Derrida famous. Deconstruction means digging down beneath these binary wars (masculine/feminine, theism/atheism, religious/secular, faith/reason, body/soul—the list is long) to unearth the forces by which these binary effects were constructed in the first place, to see what is *going on* down below.

Truth to tell, the ground of being is both he and she, masculine and feminine, if you are in need of a symbol, and neither, *ne uter*, neutral, if you are trying to avoid confusing the symbol with what it is the symbol of. But *neutral* also sounds horrible because it makes God sound like an impersonal "it," which is *less* than a person, whereas for theists God is ultrapersonal and in Christianity, three times over, although Buddhists would have no trouble with it ("it"). So this puts the Abrahamic-biblical tradition in a bit of a bind. We lack a proper pronoun for God who is neither *he* nor *she* nor *it*. Once again, blame the bridge-builders. Their search for a Supreme Being on High, the Supreme Somebody, 𝕲𝖔𝖉, who is like us except infinitely more powerful, good and intelligent, is the source of the trouble. The personification forces us to assign a gender. Our Father? Our Mother? Our what? And that is not the end of it—this Supreme Somebody then "speaks" *back* to *us* (the Word of God), which only adds to the problem. This is the mythologization, the right religious and theological response to which, Tillich said, is atheism.

But, remember, we are not trying to detonate theism but to dig into it to see *what is going on*. The personification is not nonsense; it is mediation, so it is important, just so long as it is recognized *as* a personification. In radical theology, the name of God is not the name of a person but of the *ground* of persons. Persons are effects of a system that manifests itself in persons. That means the ground is not *less* than a person but *deeper*, not *im*personal, as if it tried to get as far as a person but failed and ended up as a poached egg or a tomato plant, but the very *source* from which persons in all their multifarious glory *emerge*.

If required to fill out a census form, the ground of being would check *every* block, all of the above—white and not so white, black and not so black, masculine and feminine and all the innumerable and unforeseeable genders, transgenders, pigmentations, and ethnicities in-between or yet to come. The ground of being is, in nuce, embryonically, both spiritual and material, terrestrial and celestial, light and dark, good and evil, peaceful and belligerent, omninamable and unnamable—the whole crazy quilt of human life, good, good, very good, Elohim is said to have said, but very shortly concluded could also turn out to be pretty bad (Gen. 6). When *persons* emerge, they represent a *manifestation* of the *power* of the *ground* of being. That is a splendid point, very beautiful, very edifying. But be not puffed up—so do dolphins (my granddaughter's choice), dinosaurs (my grandson's), oceans (my choice), acorns and insects, streetlights and stars, nebulae and neutrinos, which vastly outnumber us and much of which preceded us and will outlast us.

The better way to put all this, the radical way, is to say that the ground of being is not *im*personal, but *pre*personal or *pro-to*personal, the very soil from which persons spring. Persons are emergent properties of the ground of being, but of a particularly interesting sort—of course, so is everything else, if you zoom in on them, one by one—where the ground of being actually takes *cognizance* of itself and comes to affirm itself, to say, yes, yes, alleluia, amen! Personhood is one of being's powers or potencies. It is that infinite depth in persons that we salute in our daily salutations—"Hello," "Good-bye," "God be with you" (he/she/it already is!).

These greetings seem casual and automatic, like a slight nod to a complete stranger passing by, but they are filled with infinite depth, with radical theological import, which is why we do not tip our hat to the fireplug as we pass it by, and why we feel slighted when we are treated like fireplugs by others. That depth is also why persons are mysterious, why people we have known all our lives are capable of surprising us, sometimes leaving us speechless—for better and, alas, sometimes for worse. Emmanuel Levinas (1906–1995), the great Jewish philosopher of this phenomenon, says that other persons are a shore we set out for but will never reach, which is the "distance" which is coconstitutive of their "proximity," for, remember, God is "not far."

■ ■ ■

Prayer. So, then, when we pray, what is going on? To whom or what are we praying? To an Invisible Magic Friend? To a Big Guy in the Sky? Can you pray to the ground of being? Prayer is deadly serious, mind you, whether you believe in God in the conventional sense or you have something else in mind. Prayer is a question of the first order if we are going to talk about God and theology. I started out my life praying like mad, praying for my life—or, more precisely, for my afterlife. Classical theologians say that there is no religion without prayer, no theology without prayer, and indeed no idea of God without prayer. I agree. On this point, I am an ultraconservative. I have been there. Where there is God, there is prayer; where there is prayer, there is (a) God, under *any* name, with or *without* God or prayer or religion in a rigid or narrow sense. Prayer and religion are coextensive: so much prayer, so much religion, and conversely.

What's this? Radical theologians pray? Like mad, I would say. But the problem is obvious. Praying is unavoidably praying to *Somebody*. How can you pray to the unconditional? Can you light a candle to the unconditional on the night before the big game? Remember what Tillich said. When we *think* about the unconditional, it is *unavoidable* that we think of *something*, and when we *pray* it is unavoidable that we pray to *somebody*, unavoidable that we would *personify* God, speak to God *as if* God were someone to speak to and have a conversation with which, in an important way, a symbolic way, I think is *true*. There is a measure of truth in everything which is or it would not be there at all.

When I alluded earlier to the Canticle of Brother Sun and Sister Moon of St. Francis of Assisi, that was not a literary flourish. Well, maybe it was, but it was not only a literary flourish. It was made in earnest, in theological—radical theological—earnest. Our conversations with God are something like the conversation St. Francis has with the sun and the moon, with the wind and the air, with water and fire, with earth and its fruits and flowers, even with death itself, which is a part of life, a part of the whole eco-theo-bio-system St. Francis is praising. No wonder, then, that its opening words served as the title of *Pope* Francis's call for global awareness about climate change. Notice that *Saint* Francis says "praised be You, my Lord, *through* [*per*]" our brothers and sisters. This is excellent pan*en*theistic language, the *per* signifying the *mediation* of the unconditional *through* conditional things like winds and waters, fruits and flowers.

But what about the "You"? That is the hard part. That is the *primal* and *underlying* personification in this canticle of personifications—of the four elements as our brothers and sisters, as siblings. We resonate with this canticle, this song, because this is something we all do, and it is serious and significant. This is the way we might talk to a backyard tree we have cared for tenderly over the years, to an old family clock that has been handed down through the generations, which still sings to us on the hour—*almost* on time, but we treasure it so dearly that we forgive it its minute trespasses in that regard.

Still, personifications are just make-believe, fantasies, at best poetic tropes! Not so fast. Remember the rule: if you understand what a symbol is, you will never say *only* a symbol. Symbols are exactly the opposite of frivolous make-believe. They demand the depth of mind and heart of a St. Francis, the spirit of a saint, the power of a poet. They are deep and artful ways we make contact with the ground of being. They originate in a recognition that these things (*Dinge*) are not just things, that there is *more* to them, and that they give us *access* to the *recess* and the *excess* of the unconditional (*unbedingt*). These things resonate with the depths.

This old clock, a family keepsake, does not simply tell the time; it tells us the story of our life, of our parents and their parents, now long dead. It sounds the hour of our death, *nunc et in hora mortis nostrae* (here the Gothic script is just right!) of Sister Death. Imagine how much inner strength and depth of mind it takes to speak of death as our sister and truly mean it. I have tried and failed, although having a sister you do not get along with is not unheard of. We cannot put a price on such things, and we do not possess them; we are possessed by them, seized by a matter of ultimate concern, which is religion in the radical sense. It is a priceless *sacrament* in a religion-less religion of the ground of being. It is an occasion for prayer, not a grabby petitionary prayer for a promotion or a Super Bowl championship, but a *meditative* one, one that stops us in our tracks, brings us up short, seizes our attention, or a prayer of gratitude for the blessing that life represents, a great and sweeping "hallelujah"— Leonard Cohen is singing as he prays, praying as he sings. As Martin Heidegger (1889–1976) said—and this translates without loss into English—radical thinking is thanking (*Denken ist Danken*). Praying is not trying to get something but letting it get us, letting go of what is preventing it from getting us, leaving ourselves exposed. Praying does not mean drawing attention to what we want to have. Praying is paying attention to what always already has us, which is not far.

In prayer, understood radically, not pietistically or formulaically or fetishistically, we make contact with the ground of being and it is with this ground that we converse, *as if* it were an old friend, which it *is*, if by a friend we mean a source of comfort, strength and solace. If a "Man of Reason"—I think of "Doc Martin" when I see this expression—objects that this is not really true, we would press this uptight fellow about what he means by *true*. Is a great work of art *true*? Or is it just make-believe? The work of art is a source of truth, but it is not true with what the philosophers call *propositional* or *representational* truth, where if I say, "S is P," or "The Liberty Bell is cracked," that represents a fact of the matter, picks out an SP out there, a cracked bell, outside my proposition. We locate novels in the fiction section of the library because the characters and the narrative are more or less fictitious. But the drama, the emotion, the insights into life and death, vice and virtue, wisdom and folly, are all true, deeply, sometimes punishingly so, not with propositional truth but with narratival truth.

Making obtuse objections to this kind of truth is why Nietzsche said that truth is a woman, a light-footed dancer upon whose feet the Man of Reason is always stepping. Thus do I speak of and to God, not as if there is an SP out there, or up there, who answers to this name, but with subtilitas, speaking as to the deepest currents of life, of the world, linking myself up with the tides and the winds of the world, with the depths of life and the darkness of death, with the grand power, the great rhythm of being which is—this is such a wonderful word—*unprethinkable*. "It" got there before I arrived on the scene. I was never consulted. Before I am, it was there. It was already there to greet me when I arrived and it will be there at the end to bid me a fond adieu, *à Dieu*, to-God, turned *to* God, turned *by* God, being *with* God, God be with you, he/she/it already is, whatever is going on in the name of God. If you pay attention.

What is prayer? Prayer is paying attention. Prayer is saying yes, amen, hallelujah. Prayer is an ear pressed close to the breast of being, an eye opened wide by the wonder of it all. Even in its most rudimentary form, when it is asking somebody for something (petitionary prayer), it is giving word to a desire, and every desire contains a desire beyond desire, a hope against hope, a love beyond being. What are we praying for? For life, for more life, for ourselves, for one another, for the earth, for all creatures great and small, whose siblings are the elements with whom we communicate in the ground of our being, with whom we celebrate, yes, yes, hallelujah, amen.

■ ■ ■

The Prayer of a Radical Theologian. Radical theology is not a literary ruse. So, yes, we *can* light a candle to the unconditional, as a beautiful symbol of light where it all seems dark, of an opening when everything is closing in on us. Who gave the clergy exclusive rights to candles? Radical theologians do pray, and, if you go by me, they pray like mad, for all their *worth*, to make themselves *worthy* of what is happening to them (Lesson Eleven). The word *prayer* comes from *precor*, from which we also get the word *precarious*. Prayer is for the precarious, for mortals like us. So, in a gesture of reversal, as a thorn in the rose that some theists pin on themselves, I would turn the tables on the them and say that they have made things easy for themselves. They have secured in advance all the conditions they need to pray, to say that their prayers to heaven rise, and to feel assured they are answered, one way or the other. They have a community with whom to pray, a name for the one to whom they pray, buildings built for prayers, one whom they assure themselves will hear their prayers, numerous prayer-guides and famous books of prayer, illuminated medieval manuscripts, which gives them tried and tested prayers, so they are not lost for words.

Aided by an ensemble of practical supports, their prayer is entirely possible, but maybe *too* possible, too safe and secure, which is why it can sometimes degenerate into routinized, rote, repetitious religiosity. But I would say that prayer is *more truly prayer* when it is more precarious, when we are bereft of such supports, left hanging without a prayer, without the comforts and accoutrements of religion, not the least bit sure that anyone is there to hear our prayers, when we are left praying that somehow somewhere our prayers are heard. I would say that prayer is truly possible only when it is *im*possible, when we have to pray just to be able to pray. A prayer is a "wounded word," as Jean-Louis Chrétien (1952–2019) says, sent up or down or all around by those who have no idea of whether or not it will get lost in the mail, like a message in a bottle to who knows where.

Once again, remember the principle of the inside/outside, this other prayer, this sense that no one is there to hear our prayer, is a common occurrence *in* confessional prayer, where the spiritual masters speak of a sense of desolation which is intrinsic to their consolation, like the famous "dark night of the soul" in St. John of the Cross, when even the saints are convinced they are atheists. Mother Teresa said as much. That confirms the ground-diggers' point: that if you dig deep enough into the tradition you will hit radical ground. The outside is already present on the inside, which is why the insiders are trying so hard to keep it out.

Derrida, who is officially an atheist—by the standards of the local rabbi or pastor—repeats in his writings almost daily, almost hourly, as if he had taken a monastic vow to observe the hours, *Viens, oui, oui*, "Come, yes, yes." He is himself a somewhat Jewish, almost messianic, slightly atheistic, quasi-Augustinian man of prayer. *Viens*, from *venir*, is the invocation, the exclamation of the "event" (*évenir, événement*), which is also the penultimate line of the New Testament (Derrida did not know that at the time he wrote it).

Viens is the prayer of the event, the event of prayer. We pray you, "come"—we who? Who are we? We are the ones who are praying like mad, praying not to get lost, praying not to get any more lost than we already are, praying that our prayers if not to heaven go, that they go somewhere. We are the restless hearts, the ones who do not know what will give them rest. We are the ones who do not know who we are. We are the blind, praying in the dark, de profundis, abyss calling out to abyss, blinded by our tears, praying and weeping, hanging on precariously by a prayer, praying to know how to pray, which is already a prayer, prayer's first prayer.

When we pray, we pray to remember that we are in the holy presence of the event that is coming to pass in the name (of) God. We are praying in response to a call we are not sure we heard. Is it really God who calls? Or the world? Or some dark unknown force, some unruly unconscious drive? Who knows who is calling? God only knows. When will you come? That is our first, last, and constant prayer. We promise we will keep you in our (quasi-Augustinian) memory, in our heart, yes, every day, yes, every hour. Come. Yes, yes. Amen.

All this I lift, with a few twists, from a man who said he "rightly passes for an atheist"! I will definitely come back to all this (Lesson Eleven). This is what I am going for.

Lesson Five

THE MYSTICAL SENSE OF LIFE

WHAT WE have said about prayer leads directly to the lesson for today, which is the mystical sense of life. This is nothing exotic. Everyone has it. If you think you do not, something is missing. Call your doctor. Maybe it will show up on an MRI. Or just keep reading, and you will see what I mean.

One of the first questions to get my attention as a young novice was the idea of "supernatural grace," which I was told comes along as a spiritual booster shot to give human nature the extra charge it needs to embrace the truths of faith. The supernatural is our share on earth in God's own nature. Grace is accidentally (as a booster shot) what God is essentially (the divine life itself). In heaven, the supernatural will be superfluous, since we will then see God face to face. Without the supernatural we would be forced to make our way on earth with "the light of unaided natural reason." So the supernatural is nature's necessary supplement (its spiritual band aid).

Fascinated, I asked the director of novices about it, and he told me to drop it. Stick to reading the lives of the saints, he said. I could take this up later on, after the novitiate, when we would be taking philosophy and theology courses in the scholasticate (college). I decided to observe my vow of obedience selectively. From the first part, the lives of the saints bit, I quietly granted myself a special exemption, but, on the second point, I obeyed Brother Director with an unnatural fury that would never leave me, to this very day, as I write, more than sixty years later.

I would eventually decide that that the supernatural is a mystification, and that it, as much as anything else, *more* than anything else, is the reason nobody trusts theology and why religion is making itself unbelievable. Supernaturalism is a kind of opticotheological illusion in which figures emerging from the depths of our experience are mistakenly described as dropping from the sky. The supernatural is a mystification of the inborn (natural) mystical sense of life, by which I mean our consciousness of unity with God. Well, make that with *what is going on* in the name of God. This was first evoked for me by the prayer we said back in the Brothers: "Let us remember that we are in the holy presence of God"—which should get your attention if you let yourself think about it. So be assured. By *mystical* I do not mean the holy hallucinations and loony levitations described in the lives of the saints that Brother Director wanted me to read. I mean a deep-set awareness of that in which we live and move and have our being, which, far from having been borne to earth by celestial powers, pretty much comes along with being born. You do not have to shop for it on Amazon. It does not arrive by overnight delivery from on high.

So, the lesson for today is to understand that we are all mystics—some more than others, of course, and some in the mode of denying it, which only proves that it is there, the way a man running from a bear bears witness to the bear, in the mode of running from it. The first order of business is to shake the *supernatural attitude*, to suspend it, because it is the source of the trouble with religion and theology. This is easier said than done because it has roots deep in an ancient psychocosmology. (Try thinking about God without looking up.) For some of us, the supernatural attitude has become second nature. But, if we can put it out of action, we will see what is *really going on* in religion, without the illusion, without the mystification, without the mythologization. And then we will be able to get at what we *really believe*, which is the radical theological point, which in this lesson we describe as the mystical sense of life.

■ ■ ■

How the Absolute Spirit Arrived in Upper Manhattan. The critique of supernaturalism is central to Tillich. One of his student dissertations was how to square this mystical sense, which means unity with God, with our sense of guilt, which means our separation from God. He resolved this in classic Lutheran style by saying that we are accepted (united) even though we are unacceptable (sinners). Cast in the language of philosophy, which Luther hated, he said we are bound up with God in the ground of our being even if we do everything we can to run from it in our everyday being, like the man running from the bear. In this lesson, I am less interested here in the break (the Lutheran guilt) than in the unbreakable bond with (what religion calls) God, without which we would not be at all, inasmuch as (the name of) God is (the name of) that in which we live and move and have our being. Now, Tillich, too, did not drop from the sky. His work goes back to Georg Hegel (1770–1831) and Schelling, who was Tillich's real muse and also Hegel's antagonist. Together, Hegel and Schelling are his intellectual deep pockets, and I will bring them up a lot in this lesson, all by way of filling in where the critique of supernaturalism is coming from and where it is leading.

Tillich is a major player in the tale I am telling because his emigration to the United States after the Nazi seizure of power in his homeland was an important milestone in the story of radical theology in the Anglophone world. Back in the turbulent 1960s, when I was a graduate student, Tillich was one of the stars in the intellectual firmament. He was a public intellectual of the first order, a University Professor at Harvard, consulted by world leaders, in dialogue with people like Albert Einstein. His *Courage to Be*, a perfectly serious theology book, was actually a popular bestseller. Today it is considered a classic and continues to be read, even as a younger generation of theologians have happily rediscovered Tillich.

In 1933, Tillich published *The Socialist Decision*, in which he criticized National Socialism as a reactionary and antimodern movement, a deluded return to a counterfeit past turning on a nostalgic conception of a time of lost greatness. Of Marxist Socialism, on the other hand, we might say its heart was in the right place except it had no heart. While it describes a future classless society, it was a soulless dialectical machine, taken up by a ruthless state apparatus, more likely to kill us than to cure us if we got in its way, all supposedly in the name of justice. Only the justice of the prophets, prophetic justice, which dreamed of a messianic age of peace, which counted every fallen tear, was worthy of the name of Socialism and of Christianity. Christianity is the true Socialism. Socialism is the true Christianity. Powerful and persuasive as it was, this proved to be an argument calculated to please nobody. The German Lutheran church did not rise to the occasion, which was disappointing, nor was it suffered gladly by the National Socialists, which was not surprising. The book cost Tillich his job at the University of Frankfurt, and, had he stayed around long enough, it would have likely cost him his life, as witness Dietrich Bonhoeffer (1906–1945). But it also earned him an invitation from Reinhold Niebuhr (1892–1971) to Union Theological Seminary in New York City.

Thus did the *Absolute Spirit*—highlight that phrase and we will see if we can unpack it—arrive like a German refugee in uptown Manhattan and learn to speak in English. Thus did radical theology make its Atlantic crossing. Having roots in *German idealism* (a term I will spare you wrestling with here), Tillich seriously thought that when he left Germany, at the age of forty-seven, holding a prestigious academic position, he considered his theological career over. Thinking that serious theology can only be done in German, in Germany, he had no idea of the career that awaited him in English, in America, in the Anglophone world. Along with Alfred North Whitehead (1861–1947) and American process theology, he supplied radical theology with its defining theoretical firepower. Its practical firepower (theology is always theo*praxis*, or it is a ruse), the existing American emancipation movements—of African Americans, of women, the Social Gospel and labor movements—were already here to welcome him at the harbor. Theopraxis means that if theology does not hit the streets, if it does not hold up traffic, it is a fake. Tillich was central to Bishop John Robinson's bestseller *Honest to God* (Lesson One) and the "death of God theology" of the 1960s.

Theologians are not necessarily saints. After his death, his wife, Hannah, published an account of his marital infidelities, and, prescient as he was about the rise of fascism in 1930s Germany, he never seemed taken by the terrible scar of racism in mid-century America. He would influence Martin Luther King Jr., Mary Daly, and James Cone, who would take this work where he did not go, into feminism and civil rights, which, alas, were never on Tillich's American radar.

Tillich's more popular books brought home in English what Hegel and Schelling had come up with. In a sophisticated and intimidating philosophical idiom, they brought God down to earth and worked out the metaphysics of what we are calling panentheism, our being-in-God, God's-being-in-us—the first step in radical theology. But do not panic. My ground-digging approach does not require digging into their punishing texts directly here, although they repay close study, if you can deal with the dazzling, dizzying discourse they call *dialectical*.

They may have been the model for Gilbert and Sullivan's spoof of the confusing sermons of mystical Germans; they are certainly the very model of a modern metaphysician. But it will not kill you to get the big picture here, an overview of the profound breakthrough they made that changed everything thereafter. If we think of *supernaturalism* as a kind of top-down, drop-from-the-sky theology, they propose—without embracing naturalism, which is the trick—a bottom-up, emerging-from-the-deep theology, which recognizes that religion grows on earth like a native vegetation. Stay with me. I promise you this all makes sense.

■ ■ ■

The Presence of God. The great English Romantic poet and literary theorist Samuel Taylor Coleridge had a taste for German metaphysics. Coleridge was convinced that an English meadow was not just a meadow in England, that it was marked with an excess, suffused with a richness, a cosmic wealth and power, that transcends Newtonian clockwork mechanics. He found in Schelling an idea of Nature (notice the caps) that was not mechanistic but organic, not dead but living, not bits of matter in motion but an immense and mobile power, filled with divine life, with the underlying power of God. Even the most commonplace things are iridescent with divine glory, an occasion for seeing God in a sunflower, not far from the soaring spirituality of St. Francis's *Laudato Si'*. Baruch Spinoza (1632–1677) had put this point perfectly, *Deus sive natura*, God or nature, which logicians call a *weak disjunction*, meaning use whichever word you prefer, or both at the same time, no need to choose between them.

The idea of Nature in Romanticism is the mystical sense of life in action in a cultural movement, a sense of the presence of God in the world, born of a midnight meditation, or of an absolutely quiet morning sunrise. God is not far. That is the beginning, the middle, and the end in radical theology, the proviso being that the name of God is here doing service for the name of that in which we live and move and have our being, and the assumption being that this experience can be accessed by anyone paying attention, under any number of other names, no need for a special communication from on high.

Hegel defined religion as our consciousness of unity with God and he said that that faith is its "immediate" form, meaning an innocent, untested, unanalyzed awareness of the presence of God. He said faith is "certain," not in the way they say it in the Bible Belt, with pupils dilated, but in the sense of a real and undeniable experience where *something is certainly going on*—just pay a visit to your nearest mountaintop or sit by the sea and listen—the question being *what*, what to call it, and *how*, how to think and respond to it.

When Tillich wrote *Dynamics of Faith*, one of his most famous books—if you have not read this book, stop everything you are doing, call in sick, and read it—that is the faith he was talking about. What Tillich decidedly did not mean is the degraded supernaturalist correlate in circulation these days, where faith is taken to mean assenting to a *creedal proposition* for which there is insufficient evidence but accepting it on the basis of the superior authority of a Supreme Being who "revealed" it to us. In order to keep faith safe from this distortion, I will call the latter *belief*. I like to think that, with no loss to his argument, Tillich could have entitled this book *Dynamics of Doubt*, on the grounds that by *faith* he meant the most sincere and sustained attention to the ground of being, under any name, which is even found in doubting the name of God by people whom the clergy would consider atheists. To the consternation of the pious, we are saved not only by faith but also by an earnest and searching doubt. That means the name of God has the status of a symbol, with all the cautionary notes attendant upon symbols discussed earlier (Lesson Two). God is unconditional, but the unconditional is not God.

You will notice that we have approached faith and religion without having said a word about surplices, Sabbath services, or supernatural interventions. Hegel, Schelling, and Tillich make everything turn on the mystical sense of unity with Nature which comes to a head in what they called *Spirit*. By Spirit they meant the cultural and historical world as distinct from the natural world, the revelation of the divine being not only in unconscious natural powers like mountain tops but also and above all in conscious human history, and most especially in art, religion, and philosophy, which are its spiritual summits, absolute Spirit. Nature and Spirit are not two different things but two sides—or, better, two stages—of the same thing. The divine being has both an inner spiritual dimension and an outer natural one, an invisible inside and a visible outside. Nature is visible Spirit, Schelling said, and Spirit is invisible Nature, and never were the twain apart. There are not two different worlds, one natural and the other supernatural, but one world in varying levels of manifestation, now as nature, now as Spirit, expressing itself now in the work of art, now in religion, now in philosophical thinking; one and the same content, emerging or revealing itself in different forms.

Spirit has not dropped from the sky; it is the unfolding of the same content whose antecedent stage was Nature. Nothing was handed down to us by a Supreme Being, who entrusted it to his vicars to keep it safe from women, gays, lesbians, heretics and other sexual and doctrinal dissidents. This experience of unity with the divine being is available to anyone who is paying attention, to poets or postal workers, to anyone aware and mindful of something humming in the background of ordinary experience, like the buzz of distant traffic, or, as Schelling put it, anyone sensitive to the inner "powers" of being, to being's interior "potencies," which are to be found anywhere we turn. Schelling said that some of these powers "dark," as in the "dark side" of the Force, which is attested to by the evil in the world. That is the side of Schelling that drew Tillich more to Schelling than to Hegel, who had a more sanguine sense that all is *ultimately* well with the world, if you take a long enough look. Schelling thought, maybe not. More about that later, as it is very important (Lesson Six).

■ ■ ■

A Paradigm Shift. By now the thought has crossed your mind that this is all very lovely, but it is basically a bunch of Romantic poets, philosophers, and theologians indulging their subjective fantasies. Not so fast. This is revolutionary stuff. Schelling knew the science of his day and was, shall we say, struck by the work being done on electricity. His work was actually quite prescient (he also helped kick-start the serious study of mythology, about which more shortly). Scientists today think in terms of fields and their excitation, electromagnetic and quantum fields, and the last thing they would say is that matter is like a bunch of inert billiard balls bouncing off each other or that quantum phenomena run like clockwork. Furthermore, when Einstein demonstrated the convertibility of mass and energy, that looked more like Schelling's theorem of the convertibility of Spirit and Nature than anything Newton proposed. Schelling was on to something new and different than the old mechanism that Coleridge, too, could not tolerate.

Philosophically speaking, Hegel and Schelling were proposing a radical paradigm shift, that we think in terms of *systems*, or, as we would say today, *networks*, or, as the physicists would say, *fields*, rather than in terms of particular objects. Do not view things in atomic isolation but see them in terms of the larger systems to which they belong, of which they are a part, in which they participate, to which they give expression. They were working out a logic of *expression*, of *manifestation*—let us say a vertical logic, from inner essence to outer manifestation, from concealed depth to surface expression. A particular object is not an atomic individual; it is a particular expression of an underlying universal system. The difference between the "speculative" philosophy of the Germans and the English empiricists is not that the empiricists kept their feet on the ground and paid attention to empirical data while the Germans had their heads in the clouds. The difference is that

Hegel and Schelling—unlike Aristotle, Newton and the empiricists—did not think in atomistic terms, in terms of *things*, and of a *linear* one-to-one causality, this causing that. Thinking like that makes "quantum entanglement" look "spooky." Ultimately, such linear thinking leads back, or rather *up*, to a First Thing, a Supreme Being, who got it all started but who was in no need of being started, to the First Cause Uncaused. That made it easy for David Hume, who shared this assumption, to express his total skepticism about getting back that far. The German metaphysicians, by contrast, thought in terms of the underlying networks to which things belong and of how things are expressions or excitations of these underlying systems or fields.

The things *we do*, we do not do in isolation as solitary agents. As a political theory, this would mean no "liberal individuals" need apply. When we do something, which we certainly do, there is also some deeper system (a community, a tradition, a language) upon whose resources we are drawing and some universal agency working itself out *in* what we do. The implications of all this for thinking about art and religion are nothing short of revolutionary, completely revising what we mean by *inspiration* and *revelation*.

Schelling and Coleridge said that what we call *inspiration* in a work of art is not the result of a supernal being whispering in our ear. It is the collaborative effect of sensuous, natural, unconscious forces working in tandem with the conscious art of the individual artist. The artwork gives form and body to the workings of the divine being (the complex of natural and cultural forces) in the world, which is making itself palpably present *in* the work. The work of art is not a copy or imitation (the classical mimesis theory) of an individual being but an *expression* of the universal Spirit (ground of being). Van Gogh is not trying to give us a good idea of what a haystack looks like in case we have never seen one. He is disclosing the *world* of the peasant, all the forces in that world, the joys and sorrows, the form of life of the peasant world, the way the powers of life and death, of being and nonbeing take shape there.

Just so, religion is not merely a matter of individual acts of piety directed at particular religious objects—representations of which were all over our house when I was growing up. That is religiosity, not what Hegel and Schelling meant by religion. Nor is it a list of do's and don'ts ultimately issuing from on high. That is pietism, not religion. The myths and symbols of religion are not meant as representations of entities in the real but invisible world. That is superstition, not religion. From the point of view of the individual, these imaginative figures of art and religion are expressions—in word and song, image and narrative—*of* our elemental bond with the ground of our being, of our consciousness of unity with God. From the point of view of the Spirit, the Spirit is taking shape *in* the world in art and religion, revealing itself as the beautiful and the holy, which are stages of its development or unfolding life. Artworks and religious symbols are not fictions that some primitive intelligence arbitrarily made up. They are reverberations from the ground of being recorded in what we call art and religion. That is the paradigm behind Coleridge's image in one of his most famous poems: religion and art are the music the winds of the Spirit play upon the "eolian harp" of our soul. That point is not to be dismissed as "mere" poetry; it is the poetic correlate to a different way of thinking, to what we call today field theory, to systems theory, and ultimately to the very idea of a paradigm shift, which is a shift in the system, in the entire way of thinking about things, not the discovery of some new entity. Copernicus did not propose any new stars but a new way of think about the stars we already knew.

This also explains what is really going on in poetic and religious *revelation*, where their genuinely *revelatory* power lies. Poets and theopoets are not simply making things up. They are making themselves available as nodular points in which all the forces of nature, language and culture are concentrated and expressed. Art and religion *reveal* a world, a form of life, a lifeworld, a mode of being-in-the-world, a characteristic understanding of life and death, of joy and sorrow, which is not just a human invention but a formation of the Spirit, created in tune with the ground of being (Spirit/Nature). Revelation does not mean a special delivery from on high that has disclosed information beyond the reach of human wit. Revelation is the self-revelation of the Spirit, and it arises from the bowels of being, revealing the inner essence of the forces with which we resonate. This has nothing to do with a clouds-parting, sky-opening-up supernatural intervention. That is the mystification of the mystical sense of life. The supernatural is not just superfluous, it is *deformative*, what Tillich called a "half-blasphemous and mythological" distortion of our bond with being. It destroys the reputation of religion and invites the scorn of the cultured despisers of theology. It deforms faith and defaces the deeply ingrained, latent, unanalyzed preconceptual understanding of that in which we live and move and have our being which makes up the mystical quality of life.

■ ■ ■

Faith and Reason. Having effectively relieved the supernatural of its duties, having pulled the plug on the war between natural and supernatural, Hegel and Schelling have also laid to rest the opposition between faith and reason, or the religious and the secular, which today has become downright dangerous. In the middle ages, faith and reason got along swimmingly. I spent my early student years studying Latin and pouring through Thomas Aquinas's *Summa Theologica*, where the theology and the metaphysics are so seamlessly woven together that I hardly noticed the difference. Even the word *secular* in the middle ages referred to the "secular masters," who were actually the *priests* who taught theology and who resented the intrusion of the new *religious* orders, the Franciscans and Dominicans, into the established ranks of the theological faculties. That, by the way, is the provenance of the religious versus secular terminology of today. In Catholic-talk, when I was a member of the De La Salle Brothers, I was "a religious" or "in the religious life," while my mother back home, pious to a fault, was "a secular."

But, in modernity, things had deteriorated. The title of Immanuel Kant's (1720–1804) book *Religion Within the Limits of Reason Alone* (1793) says it all. Kant held that religion boiled down to rational ethics, and that the rest of religion, like prayers and rituals, was irrational superstition and should be boiled off. Kant stressed the purity of reason, which made reason sound unbelieving, while the Protestant theologians reacted by stressing the purity of faith, which made faith sound like blind and irrational feeling. So theology ended up looking superstitious and philosophy rationalistic. The two sides retreated to their respective corners, and what was once a distinction became an invidious divide that has lasted until today, where it has gotten even worse.

Hegel thought that if you think two things are opposed, you are not thinking hard enough. Whenever you find two mortal opponents—like faith and reason—each side is being one sided, distorted. On the one hand, he thought, the theologians have to stop *mystifying* what they called *revealed truths*, like the Trinity and the Incarnation, stop declaring them off-limits to philosophy, as if they contained supernatural information otherwise withheld from natural reason. They are instead what Hegel called a *Vorstellung*, an imaginative figuration, which Tillich called "symbols," like a striking poem or painting, and it is there that everything interesting and important in religion is going on, where the *life* of the *Spirit* is on full display and found in its most vivid form. They are not off-limits to philosophers (as matters of revelation) but *imaginative figures* fresh from the wellsprings of experience providing important clues and pointers provoking philosophical thought about the ultimate make up of reality. Religious matters are matters for thought, daring us to *think* through what we feel in our bones, to reason through what is resonating *in* these imaginative figures.

On the other hand, the Enlightenment philosophers were singularly flat-footed or ham-fisted when it came to thinking.

They were hamstrung by a narrow idea of "reason" as a kind of abstract, lifeless logic-chopping, which Hegel called *Verstand*, translated as understanding, meaning calculative-conceptual thinking. This does violence to the mystical sense of life, mishandling its delicate fabric, missing its fine movements, degrading the inner feeling of the presence of God in the world into worthless wooden proofs for the existence of the Supreme Being (which invites skepticism about their validity). The doctrine of the Trinity, he said, leaves these clumsy knights of Verstand dumbfounded, left to counting on their fingers, one, two, three. They lack the eyes to see, *not* with the eyes of supernatural faith, of course, but with the vision afforded by a *richer idea of reason*, which Hegel called *Vernunft*. By this Hegel meant the power to *read* the *movements* of the *Spirit* in the world, to see not abstract isolated entities but a concretely self-transforming Spirit moving through its various formations, from its first appearance in the natural world into its fulfillment and completion in the workings of the human spirit (absolute Spirit).

The symbols of religion neither require supernatural legitimation nor are susceptible to rationalistic delegitimation. We need, as Coleridge said, to "suspend our disbelief" in these figures (factually they are unbelievable, like Shakespeare's ghosts) in order to understand *what is going on* in them. But we also need to suspend our belief in Pure Reason, which strikes an uncomprehending and dismissive attitude toward them. These symbols have their *own* authority and intelligibility; they have the force of the gripping vision we encounter in a work of art or a parable. This requires a hermeneutic subtilitas, an ear sensitive to what is sounding from the depths before it is drowned out—whether by Bible-thumpers back in the Bible Belt or Vatican secretaries sitting behind big desks on the one hand, or by clumsy Enlightenment rationalists on the other, the ones Nietzsche mocked as maladroit courtesans, noisily clanking about in the face of the feminine finesse of the Spirit.

The lesson is simple. Unless we lose the supernaturalism and lose the rationalism, unless we desupernaturalize and derationalize, we will not gain access to what is *really going on* in religion. *Crucify* the pretensions of theology to be the Queen of the Sciences, as it was in the middle ages, which made philosophy its handmaiden and cost many a heretic their head, and *criticize* the pretensions of philosophy which promoted the rule of Pure Reason in modernity, posing as the Supreme Court of all that is, which ridiculed religion and cost a lot of colonized peoples their head.

One way to sum all this up is simply to say that, in radical theology, the invidious distinction between *supernatural faith* and *natural reason* is demystified by being replaced by the more peaceful distinction between the *poetic* and the *prosaic*. That breaks the grip of supernaturalism without falling into naturalism. Revelation happens as a poetics, a theopoetics, which resonates with the depths, preconsciously, preconceptually, prepropositionally, in song and story and symbols, not in syllogisms. Art, religion, and philosophy (the realm of absolute Spirit)—that means a poetic, a theopoetic, and a careful hermeneutic, and we need them all. They are all stages of the same thing, three different formations of one and the same Spirit, the same content taking shape in three different forms.

■ ■ ■

Dare to Think Radically. Here, in what Hegel and Heidegger simply call *Denken* ("thinking"), we meet the principle we stated at the start (Lesson One) under the heading of the double dare: dare to think radically, which requires *both* philosophers who dare to think without fear of hitting theological ground *and* theologians who dare to theologize without fear of hitting radical ground. Radical thinking requires a new species of philosophers and theologians, willing to take the bet, unafraid of doing business together (unlike the old ones).

Daring to think includes daring to think religious symbols. Whatever the difference between Hegel and Schelling may be (next lesson), they both understood philosophy to include the *thoughtful rendering* of religious symbols, a point that is also recognized by serious theologians, who also have their own doubts about supernaturalism. Having taken down the barbed-wire barriers to revealed theology, having defused the pretense to pure reason, radical theology is positioned *to think* what is going on in religion and revelation—*as far as that is possible.* Just *how far* possible is the part where Hegel and Schelling parted company (Lesson Six).

On this point, Tillich, and we along with Tillich, take our lead from Schelling, not Hegel. Their differences, which make all the difference for radical theology, were first recorded for us in the work of a brilliant if somewhat haunted, unhappy young man from Copenhagen. He had just broken his engagement to be married back home and was in the audience in 1841 at the University of Berlin, drowning his sorrows in Schelling's lectures on religion. His name? Søren Kierkegaard (1813–1855).

Lesson Six

WHO DO THEY SAY JESUS IS?

ONE WAY to see where this paradigm shift and this dare-to-think thing is taking us is with Jesus. Where I grew up, you did not dare much with Jesus, who, according the fourth gospel, is the eternal logos, and pretty much literally did drop from the sky. Only gradually was I able to loosen up on this and get to the point where I dared to distinguish Yeshua—his Aramaic name, the real man who walked the dusty roads of Galilee—from Jesus, at the sound of whose name knees will bend (and heads, unhappily, have been knocked). So the lesson for today is Jesus, where we can see in no uncertain terms where we are being led by radical theology, by the mystical sense of life, and by the dual critique of supernaturalism and naturalism we have been discussing. Once again, this is just *my* example, drawn from my experience, and, once again, my wager is that anyone, in any culture, could conduct an analogous reflection upon the roots, the radix, of the paradigmatic stories and iconic figures they have inherited, upon what is *going on* there, which is the part that they can *really believe*, which is what I mean by *radical theology*.

If we dare to think, how dare we think of Jesus? How far dare we go? Let us ask the question Jesus puts to Peter, "Who do you say I am?" (Matt. 16:16). This is a test case of everything we are saying so far, and it is likely to set the hair on fire of a lot of people from Nashville to Vatican City. How do we approach Jesus without *supernaturalizing* him like fourth-century Greek councils or *naturalizing* him like modern philosophers? If we get this, we will get quite a lot of what we are going for in radical theology. We will be halfway there—the other half is Lessons Seven to Twelve. So don't stop reading!

■ ■ ■

What Is Emerging from the Deep? Let us start by pressing Hegel and Schelling further about just *what is going on* in religious symbols. *What* is emerging from the depths, seeking to be expressed, groaning to be born, trying to get itself *expressed*? The unconditional, the ground of being, the absolute, of course. Or, as they would say, a formation of the Spirit (*Geist*). *Geist* is such a great word that it worked its way into English; we do not have to translate it, just listen to it, as in *Zeitgeist*, the spirit of the age. The French translation has also become good English, as in *esprit de corps*, or "team spirit." Now add the German metaphysics and stir, as in *Weltgeist*, the Spirit of the world, lying at the foundations of the world, which is pretty much what *panentheism* means. The decision of earlier

English translators to render *Geist* as "mind" was mindless. It killed the Spirit.

What, then, is the Spirit? The first thing is that the Spirit is not somebody who answers to the name "Spirit," a caricature that Slavoj Žižek calls the "scarecrow" Hegel. If we did a roll call of all present, Spirit would be reported absent. If we did a census of the Spirit of the age—say, of the Roaring Twenties— the Spirit would never be counted. The Spirit is not a particular person or thing. It does not enjoy a *separate* existence. It runs *through* and is found *in* everything—the arts and sciences, the ethics and economics, the fashions and politics of the day—even as the latter exhibit, possess, or *have* the Spirit. The Spirit has all of them, and they all have the Spirit, both together, inseparably. Indeed, these are one and the same phenomenon, viewed from two different sides. Think of the Spirit as the wave of enthusiasm that rushes through a stadium of people rooting for the home team. Notice that the word *enthusiasm*, from *en + theos*, being filled with the divine (Spirit), is a kissing cousin to the word *panentheism*, the Spirit in all, all in the Spirit. Panentheism inspires pan-enthusiasm, or so it should, if you have the Spirit.

The Spirit cannot present itself in person. Then find a person in whom the Spirit is present—palpably, paradigmatically. That will provide an intuition of what is going on in the Spirit.

See where this is going? Enter: Jesus.

■ ■ ■

So, What About Jesus? The dispute between naturalism and supernaturalism, a dichotomy in desperate need of dissolution, was on full display in the early nineteenth century. The Enlightenment dared to criticize the supernatural Jesus, but, blinded by its rational light, it could not see any further. It treated Jesus condescendingly, patting him on the head as the model of the good and brave man who died for speaking truth to power. Jesus, Kant thought, is an exemplary man, a great example of the philosophical point Kant was independently making about the moral law back in the philosophy department. Confronted with religious scriptures the Enlightenment behaved like a book reviewer who fact-checks a novel and concludes with no little satisfaction that the novelist obviously made up the story. Jesus did not really walk on water, but on big rocks at water level. Thomas Jefferson had a copy of the New Testament in which he had taken a pair of scissors to the miracle stories (Christian Nationalists think that is fake news fabricated by the liberal media). Would Jefferson have done the same thing to the ghosts in Hamlet and Macbeth? That hatchet (or scissors) job is the best that pure reason can do with Jesus. Anything else stumps it, which means it gets stamped as "irrational" and Jesus ends up on the cutting room floor of the Enlightenment. Hegel and Schelling loudly objected to treating Jesus so poorly. We do not need Jesus for an example of a good man, they said; we already have Socrates for that. "What would Socrates do?"

But if, heaven forbid, we do not want to diminish Jesus by naturalizing him as an earthman, how on earth can we take him seriously without supernaturalizing him as a heavenman? Enter the paradigm switch. Hegel thought everything really interesting about Jesus is found not in the Jesus of (factual) history but in the *story*, where he is not just another *man*, like Socrates, not just a brave man, but a *God-Man*.

But wait! Has Hegel conceded that Jesus as a God-Man is something supernatural? Not a bit. Hegel is saying that Jesus is a Vorstellung—an *icon* (Col. 1:15), a symbol, a poem, a visible figure of the invisible Spirit, who provides us with an *intuition* of what is *going on* in the divine life of the Spirit. Hegel is not distinguishing the Jesus of (rational) history from the Christ of supernatural faith. His work had attracted the attention of David Strauss (1808–1874), whose *Life of Jesus* (1835) was published four years after Hegel's death, having come to Berlin to study under Hegel the very year that Hegel would die. Strauss thought that Hegel has made the breakthrough with his notion of a Vorstellung, which Strauss employed to say that the stories in the New Testament are exactly that, stories (*mythos*), in which, after his death, Jesus of Nazareth is raised up into imaginative space. What Hegel called a Vorstellung Strauss called the "mythical point of view." Hegel is effectively distinguishing the prose of concepts from the poetics of the Vorstellung, the Jesus of *Historie*, the rigorously disciplined factual account, from the Jesus of *Geschichte*, the living history, what is *really happening* in this *figure*, what is really *inspiring* in this figure of the Spirit, of which Jesus is the palpable embodiment (incarnation), indeed the very paradigm, the *greatest imaginative figure* ever. His physical death under Pontius Pilate, the little we know of him recorded in the history books, is purely *prosaic*, propositional, factual information (like what we know of the original King Arthur), all of which left to itself would have simply been ignored or forgotten by history. What lived on was the *poem*, the theopoem. I myself have pinned my account of radical theology to a scene on the Areopagus which scholars say likely never took place. *So what?* King Lear did not exist. Ancient Athena did not exist—and look what she in*spired*. Radical theology is a theology of "so what?" (Chapter Twelve).

In the New Testament, the mortal man, the healer, the exorcist, and the prophet, who is largely lost in the fog of history, *has been lifted up into imaginative (theopoetic) space.* There he lives forever. There they killed him but he would not stay dead— that is, they could not kill the *poem*, the *figure of the Spirit* that *emerged* in him, that burned white hot in him. There he heals the lame, performs works of wonder, and walks on water, to which the rationalists and the supernaturalists alike are tone deaf. C. S. Lewis's (1898–1963) claim that Jesus was either a liar, a lunatic, or the Lord (summarily put) is either lame or ludicrous or lousy with literalism and on my shortlist of the most tone-deaf arguments in the history of theology. We would expect more of an Oxford professor of literature and the author of *The Chronicles of Narnia.* Had he no inkling that Jesus was a *poem*, for heaven's sake? The naturalists, who rationalize these texts, and supernaturalists, who literalize them, are alike in lacking an ear for a *story*; they have no hermeneutic skills, no subtilitas. They fall for the *mystification* and miss the *manifestation* (revelation), what Hegel called the "mediation," contained in the story of the extraordinary birth (attended by angels in the infancy narratives), life (the exorcisms, the miracles), death (Good Friday, darkening of the sky), resurrection (Easter, empty tomb, new life), and aftermath of Jesus (the post-Easter stories) culminating in Pentecost, when Jesus *sends his "Spirit"* to abide in the community. This is an imaginative figuration of a ground-breaking and game-changing intuition of the divine life, of what is going on in the beating heart of being, in the ground of being, in the truth of being, in the *Spirit*. The Spirit was *in* Jesus, and Jesus is the revelation *of* the Spirit.

In radical theology, the *truth* of the Spirit is *theopoetic*. To literalize the miraculous births, deaths, and healings in the New Testament, as if the "good news" were a news report, is to make them merely *unbelievable*. The mystification invites demystification, dismissing it as so much fiction or fantasy. *Literalized*, the *bodily* Jesus would have attained orbital altitude and spent the last two millennia circulating around the earth, using his divine powers to dodge the occasional meteor. In 1950, Pope Pius XII doubled down on this problem, compounding it by declaring "infallibly" that mother Mary had *also* been *bodily assumed* into heaven! Quite an assumption! The mystification (supernaturalism) and the demystification (naturalism), stand on the same ground, prosaic propositional ground, alike in their literalization, each one as one-sided as the other, engaging in an artless tug of war brought on by their mutual inability to *read*. If you want to read the New Testament, learn how to *read a story*.

■ ■ ■

So, What Is the Revelation? The *insight* that *God is not an alien being*, although we are alienated from God. Emmanuel. God with us. God is not far. God, the kingdom of God, is within us and we are in God. Jesus was intensely sensitive to the presence of God within himself and within the world, in mustard seeds and leavened bread and wedding parties. His was a mystical sensibility of unique depth, an acute awareness of the "powers," dark and light, demonic and celestial. His vision was of God's coming triumph over the powers of darkness, the coming of God's rule in the world, of what the world was going to look like when God ruled, not the powers and principalities (the Romans). That is what he meant by "heaven," the rule *on earth* (N. T. Wright) of the heavenly powers. (Jesus had never read Plato.)

That is what is *really happening*, what there is to believe, the big story, the heart of Christian revelation, the breakthrough made in the iconic figure of Jesus, articulated in a set of moving images and memorable narratives. This insight, Hegel and Schelling said, simmered only obscurely, in a sleepy, hazy, unconscious, or preconscious form, still confused and rudimentary, even a kind of drunken stupor, in the "nature religions," still in a state of nature, in their *mythology*. There the divine life was felt beating in the power of the sun, sea, and thunder. These religions rocked in unison with the rhythms of the earth, with the seasons of nature, the seasons of life, communicating in their bones, viscerally, with the powers of being. *But* they could not quite clear their heads, sober up, shake off their somnambulance, wake up, and say it, see it, write it down, bring to words, to the Word, the Logos made flesh in a man. That takes place in *revelation*, which is a higher formation of the Spirit, of which mythology is an antecedent preparatory stage.

Hegel and Schelling thought the breakthrough beyond these purely natural processes to the *holiness* of God took place in Judaism, the religion of the *sublime*. There the grip of the religion of nature was broken, and the transcendence of the Spirit broke out, but Judaism went too far by treating the Spirit as an alien power and law. The "pagans" who came the closest to the unity of the divine and the human were the Greeks, by whom Hegel was fascinated up to the point of actually being tempted to say that it was the Greeks, not the Jews, who were the true antecedents of Christianity. The Greeks appreciated the *beauty* of the divine being in the human form (the religion of the *beautiful*) but their polytheism blinded them to the underlying unity. The Jews saw the unity and sublimity of the divine being but their sense of God's transcendence blinded them to God's immanence in the world.

The true and complete *revelation* takes place in the *story* of the Incarnation, which reveals the *unity* of immanence and transcendence, the beautiful and the sublime, the natural and the spiritual, the world and God. God is not an alien being, but the underlying Spirit *of* the world. This we learn by reading the New Testament not with the eyes of a reductionistic, rationalistic reason (*Verstand*), which takes its *scissors* to the story, and not with the eyes of supernaturalistic faith, which *reifies* the story and reduces religion to magic and superstition, but with the eyes of *Vernunft*, which *reads* the story, reads the movement of the Spirit in the story, which is *what is going on* in the biblical narratives.

Revelation means that this insight achieves clarity, sobers up, clears its head, is completed, and brought to fulfillment. This takes place in Christianity, in the radical *theopoetic* figure, the central Vorstellung, the highest symbol, the richest icon, the primary poem, the soaring theopoetics of the *God–Man*, which is, to cite the title of a famous 1965 film, "the greatest story ever told." Here we have an intuition of the divine life that flows through all things and comes into self-consciousness, self-realization, in human life, in which the "absolute Spirit" takes shape. Christianity is the *truth* of the *Spirit*, the higher *reconciling unity* of all oppositions, which Hegel called the *Aufhebung*, literally, uplifting, the least bad translation of which is probably "sublimation," which means "lifting up" the two opposing sides into a higher unity. As long as we think two things are opposites, we are not thinking hard enough. As Thomas Merton once said, we rejoice to learn that the Eternal Word has joined the human race.

■ ■ ■

The Death of God. "Good Friday" is thus the *symbol* of an *ontological* event, a "speculative" event of the greatest importance, which enacts in a drama what an old Lutheran hymn called the "death of God." The phrase caught fire in the 1960s—it even made it onto the cover of *Time* magazine (April 8, 1966) and the late night talk shows—when an American "death of God" movement (Thomas Altizer, William Hamilton and others) picked it up. That is an important and inaugural moment in the history of radical theology in the United States, but a highly controversial one. As a reading of Hegel, it was a half-truth, maybe less than half. Approaching Hegel through the eyes of Friedrich Nietzsche (1844–1900), they advanced the idea of a "Christian atheism," which sounds like the theological atheism of Tillich (Lesson One), but it was a great deal more Nietzsche than Tillich or Hegel. For Hegel himself, Good Friday meant the death of the alien being, the negation of the negation—of God, the distant God/Father as an alien power—which is a negative moment in the ongoing *life* of God, of God's coming-to-be-among-us, *Emmanuel*. It was the death of the alien being, not of the ground of being.

For Hegel, it was necessary for Jesus to *die* in order that the Spirit could move past its incarnation in a particular man to become the universal *living spirit* of All (*pan*). That is why the highest feast day on the liturgical calendar for Hegel and Schelling is neither Good Friday nor Easter but Pentecost Sunday, when Jesus returns to his Father and *sends his Spirit to dwell among us*. That is the *absolute truth* told to us—now here's the punch line—in the form of a *story*, the *greatest story* ever told. We see this pointedly in the anger of Dostoevsky's Grand Inquisitor. *We* are in charge now, not you, the furious Lord Cardinal says to Jesus, outraged that Jesus would *come back*. *We* get to say who lives and dies, not you! (Jesus met this fury with a kiss, which totally disarmed this terrible man.)

■ ■ ■

Christocentrism. If Hegel and Schelling can be faulted for anything on this point, it would not be that they attacked revelation, but that they were excessively Christocentric about it. They were supplying not just Coleridge but colonialism, Eurocentrism, and anti-Semitism with a metaphysical backup. They suspended supernaturalism but not supersessionism. By calling pre-Christian religion "mythological," they obscured its revelatory power, and by calling Christian religion "Revelation," they obscured its mythological status. They said Christian Revelation is the absolute truth, located, conveniently enough right here in the University of Berlin, the absolute center of the absolute Spirit, meaning Christian European culture. Historically, that is actually a novel idea. Europe used to be the sticks, the outskirts of Greco-Roman civilization, where you got assigned if you fell out of favor with the emperor.

The mistake Hegel and Schelling make is to fail to see that one culture's revelation is another's mythology. *Every* culture has its own set of such symbols, a *special* revelation that is special for *them*, in which their insights into what matters most to them, their form of life, are concentrated. We need to undermine both supernaturalism and its attendant supersessionism and take the theological wind out of the sails of colonialism and anti-Semitism. In its place we put a multicultural rainbow coalition—seen today in the proliferation of studies of Indigenous or first world religions—of diverse expressions of something-we-know-not-what, something that is not a thing, something that cannot be shut up in a word or a thing, intimating the ultimate condition under which words and things take place. That is the unprethinkable, the unconditional, the unconditionally unprethinkable, in which we live and have our being. (There's a line to drop at happy hour if anyone asks you what you are reading these days.)

While all this Christocentrism brought a smile to the face of the Prussian minister of religion, we cannot forget that they meant that Christianity was still a *story*, albeit the greatest story, the central Vorstellung, the highest symbol, poetics, or narrative, which stood in need of further thought. They were saying that when you get to Jesus and Christianity, don't stop. *Keep thinking!* Dare to think some *more*. That part would be likely to elicit a frown had the minister stayed around long enough to hear the second half of the lecture. They think of religion in general, both pre-Christian and Christian, as a profound but *still sensuous manifestation* of a deeper philosophical truth. Schelling speaks of a "philosophical religion," a philosophy *of* Christian revelation in the sense of unfolding the explicit philosophical content of what is revealed in symbolic form in Christianity itself. He thinks Christianity is "revealing" in the sense that, once someone points something out to you—say, a constellation in the stars: a Big Dipper here, a Great Bear there—you can thereafter see it with your own eyes (philosophy).

Hegel went *further*. When Hegel spoke of religion as a Vorstellung, a figurative, imaginative representation, he was saying that religion is philosophy cut to fit the form of those who are not cut out for philosophy. Religion is philosophy for the people—those who cannot understand philosophy itself. Christianity is the absolute truth (the "pagans" never got this far), but it is true with a truth that *only the philosophers* truly get (the Christians in the pew never get this far). It is not in the pulpit but back in the philosophy department (especially the one at the University of Berlin) where the real logic of the logos, the way the Absolute unfolds its deep laws in nature and in history, gets spelled out. Philosophy figures out what is only being imaginatively figured (Vorstellung) in art and religion. Hegel rank-orders art, religion, and philosophy, the sensuousness of art at the bottom, the conceptual thinking of philosophy at the top, religion in the middle, more conceptual than art, more sensuous than philosophy, mediating between them. They are ordered by their increasing proximity to the *Begriff*, the Concept, in caps, which sizes up and seizes (*greifen, capere*) everything that is going on in them, where God comes to know Godself, becoming Aristotle's self-thinking thought right here in downtown Berlin.

■ ■ ■

Schelling Puts His Foot Down. Nowadays we might say, in the Hegelian Concept thinking gets its head around the unconditional. That is where Schelling puts his foot down. *Nein*, not so, Schelling said. No matter how fast it is on its feet, thinking is always too little and too late. Religion and art can be interpreted, but they cannot be sublimated or transcended. They cannot be saturated by thought, which only gets so far, and, no matter how far it gets, Being is always already there. Thinking can never get there in time to lay down the conditions under which the unconditional—being—is. The unconditional is the *unprethinkable* (this wonderful word again), the *that-it-is-rather-than-not*, the existence that precedes essence. Thinking is always already breached by being. Reason is ec-static, meaning ex-posed to the unprethinkable.

This critique opened the door for Kierkegaard to get off some of his best lines against Hegel. Through the mouthpiece of his pseudonyms, Kierkegaard pilloried Hegel, unleashing a flood of witty, biting, brilliant barbs that created the scarecrow Hegel. On Hegel's view, he said, God became man in order to arrange a consultation with German philosophers about the makeup of the divine nature. He called Hegel the "absolute professor," and he said that before engaging a Hegelian in conversation we must first secure his assurance that he is only a human being. Kierkegaard possessed a pitiless wit, which was valuable up to a point—when I was young, Kierkegaard captivated me—but it ultimately distorted Hegel's image for the next century and a half. Truth to tell, Hegel was more radical than Kierkegaard, whose actual theology was quite orthodox (think of Karl Barth). He emphasized the classical transcendence of God, despite his fierce anticlericalism and antiestablishmentarianism about the Danish Lutheran church and his acute sensitivity to the existential condition of human life, which is his most lasting contribution.

In radical theology, we take our cue first from Hegel (religion is a Vorstellung) and then from Schelling's critique of Hegel (for which we have no Concept). As Kierkegaard said, we have no such gigantic head for the Absolute Concept. Religion is a sensuous symbol for which we lack the supersensuous concept, a figure we cannot finally figure out, which thought cannot ultimately transcend. This does not leave us without a clue; it leaves with *only* clues, hints, symbols, icons, traces, fingers pointing at the moon and the stars, wondering what is what, affirming an existence whose essence ever eludes us (enter

Kierkegaard). It does not leave us without a prayer; it leaves us with *only* prayers. It does not leaves us lost for words but only lost for a Final Word. It throws us back on words that vibrate in unison with the ground of being, poetic words which resonate below the radar of the Concept. We seek to dress down philosophy and its Concept, in caps, decapitate and decapitalize it, take it down a peg or two, relieve it of its puffed-up condition, and confess that we are all just mortals feeling around in the dark. *What remains are the stories*, endlessly reinterpreted, endlessly retold, endlessly recontextualized, endlessly reverberating with the power of being in ways which leave us not speechless but unable to say what is going on in any *final* way, not silencing but multiplying our discourses, forcing us to move back and forth between the prosaic and the poetic in search of an interpretation.

I should also add that, unlike Hegel, Schelling called the ground of being a "dark ground," like the "dark side" in *Star Wars*, or the underside of the divine being, or like Yahweh showing only his backside to Moses, the *posteriora dei*, the hindquarters of God, the *deus absconditus*, as Luther called it, ultimately impenetrable to thought, ultimately unprethinkable. About that, we radical theologians think—along with Kierkegaard, Heidegger, Tillich, and most twentieth-century continental European philosophers—Schelling was right. This was the Schelling that attracted Tillich, whose sense of twentieth-century history as rocked with anxiety, doubt, and meaninglessness was shaped by his experience as a military chaplain at Verdun and the Nazi nightmare in his native Germany. (From a different point of view, and for what it is worth, physicists

today think that about 94 percent of the universe is in the *dark!*)
As Tillich said, the only *nonsymbolic* thing we can say about the
unconditional is that everything we say about the unconditional
is a symbol. At bottom, there is always the mystical sense of life,
the *mysterium tremendum et fascinans,* the mystery of the unconditional, the unprethinkable, the concealed depths, the unlit
core of things running in the background. I like to say that radical theology is a Hegelianism-without-a-Concept, a kind of
headless Hegelianism, where we always and already, inescap-
ably and unsurpassably, have to do with figures and symbols,
which go all the way down (and all the way up), constituting a
poetics, where theology regroups as *theopoetics*. We seek the
unconditional, Novalis said, but everywhere we turn, we run
into conditions.

SECOND WEEK

Lesson Seven

SUPPOSE EVERYTHING JUST VANISHED?

THE STRING *Quartet.* When the *Titanic* was sinking, there was a string quartet on board that continued playing throughout the panic and the chaos. These four musicians did not abandon their instruments and run for the nearest lifeboat. In the face of certain doom, they just kept playing their music. But, if they were willing to sacrifice their lives, why not spend their time helping others get into the lifeboats? They had no idea that they would become famous for this, that they would play a poignant part in a popular American film, that anyone would ever know what they did, and they certainly did not think this generous act would earn them a boost in salary for their next engagement.

Why did they continue to play their music? That is the unsettling setting for today's lesson and the second half of the argument.

■ ■ ■

Angel Envy. When I was a young Brother, I suffered from angel envy. I even wrote my master's thesis on Thomas Aquinas's angelology. Pure spirits who lived forever united with God in eternal happiness—what's not to envy? I have since gotten over wanting to live forever, and I am disinclined to being disincarnated, but I would not object to being reincarnated two or three times, which I will point out from time to time. The first time around I would like to come back as a theoretical cosmologist, a physicist studying the origins and the destiny of the cosmos from the Big Bang to, well, God knows what.

I bring all this up for a purpose. I admit that I am getting old, but I have not lost track of the discussion. In the first six lessons, we learned that we are all in the same boat together, praying like mad for something, we know not what, under the name of the unconditional. But now, in Lesson Seven, we learn that in the meantime our ship has hit an iceberg.

So, the lesson for today starts off with a question that may, at first sight, seem out to sea. What if the *Titanic* is a cosmic symbol? What if everything, the entire universe, is like the *Titanic*, headed for the bottom—*and* we forgot the lifeboats? What if the cosmos is destined for dark, cold extinction? Odd as it may seem—bear with me—it is with this question that we begin the transition to the second stage of the argument for radical theology. It is thus we learn to wean ourselves of the inclination to speak of God in terms of being, not only of the Supreme Being but also of the ground of being, on the grounds that even the ground of being may not be all it is cracked up to be. (*Cracked up* may be an unfortunate choice of words!) In the process we will come to see that, as bad as this all may sound, it is the basis of the good news in radical theology.

In short, if the universe is like the *Titanic*, will anyone ever sign up for the string quartet?

■ ■ ■

Why Is There Nothing at All Rather than Something? Hegel put the case for the ground-diggers in an interesting way. He said that the bridge-builders' attempt to span the distance from the finite to the infinite is futile; it requires crossing an infinite expanse, and good luck with that. Instead of that exercise in futility, Hegel proposed an exercise in fertility, to let the finite "vanish" into the infinite, on the grounds that the infinite is not off in the distance but the ground on which we already stand. As being-itself is infinite and inexhaustible, the non-being of what is finite must be allowed to vanish into being-itself. In saying "vanish" he was not proposing some kind of nihilistic denial of particular things in space and time. He just wanted to make us appreciate the transient reality of finite things and the inexhaustible reality of their underlying, unifying, infinite substance—the Spirit of things—from which all particular things emerge and into which they return.

That brings out something important about panentheism. Up to now we have been emphasizing (and admittedly enjoying!) the shock that panentheism delivers to the orthodox, which they think is atheism, which they think is horrible, as did young Brother Paul and I, back in the day. But panentheism maintains a deep *alliance* with classical theism that the latter, in its panic, failed to appreciate. The panentheists never question the classical names of God—eternal being and truth, inexhaustible goodness and beauty. Their innovation is to *transfer* these eternal celestial funds to an earthly account, held here in space and time, which leaves a lot of classical theists rending their garments and looking up to heaven for relief. But while these names have changed their mailing address, they retain their validity, now for Spirit in the world, for a sacred but now entirely cosmic Spirit (*Weltgeist*). What is eternal and inexhaustible is the eternity and inexhaustibility of *this* world, for there is only one world, where it is working out its eternal being by becoming divine in space and time, which is the panentheist transcription of Divine Providence. In radical theology, that is a first step, a powerful but penultimate position. It is getting warm, but it is not there yet.

Now we come to the iceberg. What if, after allowing beings to vanish into being-itself, as Hegel counsels, being-itself also simply vanishes? What becomes of the unconditional if there is nothing at all? Does not the unconditional mean, by its very definition, unconditionally *necessary* being? But, then, what if everything vanished?

What would ever possess someone to think such a thing?

This is the widely held hypothesis of contemporary physicists. If we adopt a cosmic perspective, then, after ten to fifteen billion years or so of interesting activity early on in cosmic history, the universe will ultimately subside into many more trillions upon trillions of increasingly boring epochs, when everything gradually vanishes, where, if we were not all already dead, we would all die of boredom. The universe is expanding at an *increasingly accelerating* rate into oblivion—not utter oblivion, of course, but oblivion enough, aging not with wisdom and grace but degenerating into an inert, dissipated, exhausted, burned-out, spent condition in which nothing happens. At that point, nothing (no thing) will be around, nobody will be around to report its disappearance, and, besides, there will be no one around to whom to report. As Philip Plait puts it in *Death from the Skies*, the universe is out to kill us, but it's nothing personal. It's out to kill everything. I recommend Plait's book, but I do not recommend taking it on a plane lest you alarm your airline attendant (as I did).

The "posthumanists" think they have an answer to this problem, not a permanent one but a fairly good work around. Like young Brother Paul, they too suffer from a bit of angel envy and would like to live like the angels. This they hope to achieve not theologically but technologically, not exactly in heaven but on the "cloud," where they hope to "upload" consciousness. There they will live maintenance-free lives, with no need for food, shelter, or clothing, and where resurrection will mean having the prudence to make a back-up copy (like the Resurrection Ships in *Battlestar Galactica*) in case of accident or death. No longer bound by biology, no longer even earthbound, they could borrow robot-bodies ("downloading") to travel about the universe as far and wide as need be. Thus would they escape the fate of mother earth before she is baked to a crisp under an ever-expanding sun. The "transhuman" age, in transition to the posthuman, is already well underway, as electronic devices increasingly invade our bodies and our minds.

All this poses the next big problem for theology, as the mystical drifts toward the mathematical and religion makes itself more and more unbelievable. This requires a new species of theologians, equipped to address progressively more disincarnate beings for whom the Incarnation would be obsolete. These posthuman beings would not be born of Adam and would not need to be saved by Jesus. They would transcend the classical distinctions theology has depended upon—not only between natural and supernatural but also between natural and artificial, human and nonhuman, living and nonliving, and even spirit and matter. That in which we live and move and have our being will turn out to be "information." The Spirit will have become a specter, a simulation, where to be is to be a coded bit. *Cogito, ergo* "sim." Was Neo pulled out of the virtual world into the real one? Or vice versa? How could we tell?

Still, even if our posthuman descendants will have found a way to have jumped this earthly ship and moved on elsewhere, that will only delay the inevitable. In an expanding universe, we eventually run out of places to run. The universe keeps moving the goalposts on us, and we are outrun by the places we are running to. Wherever these posthumans might venture, this is the fate of every planet in our solar system, of every star and galaxy. Eventually, over stretches of time and space that beggar the imagination, for which mathematicians have to invent new notations just to keep count, the expansion of the universe will have overtaken everything, and things will sink into a cosmic abyss. Then Brother Sun and Sister Moon will sigh, in concert with the entire cosmos, *Dies Irae*, and Sister Death will step up and announce that she is all in all, as the world dissolves in ashes.

G. W. Leibniz (1646–1716), another of the great German philosophers, asked: Why is there something and not, rather, nothing at all? That is a mind-bending, border-breaching question. It is the puzzle addressed by the multiple creation stories found across the several religious traditions. I often used it in class to get the students' attention, which was easier to do before smart phones made it harder to produce smart students. But now we find ourselves up against another, no less mind-bending counterquestion: Why *will there be nothing* at all rather than something? Needless to say, this is bad news for all our sisters and our cousins throughout the universe, and somebody is going to have to tell Plato. He took the sun to be inextinguishable and so a similitude of the eternal being of the Forms. Wrong on both counts—instead of inextinguishable light and eternal life, cold, dark, formless death. We set out in search of the unconditional, but God knows we never expected this—no thing, nothingness, *rien, nada, nihil, Nichts,* everything having vanished (into a state of unusable entropic dissipation).

This is not a crazy conspiracy theory cooked up on the Internet, not a lie, not an outlier. This is a prominent— probably even the dominant—view of physicists today. But the science is not in yet; it is not the only possibility and not the only view. It all depends upon what dark energy decides to do, or not do, or undo, and about that we are, by definition, in the dark. Nothing says that the prevailing view will not be over-turned tomorrow morning by some newly minted PhD in physics working in a patent office somewhere because she cannot find a teaching job. Maybe, as many scientists think, there are multiple universes, a series of endless universes. Maybe, although they formulate this in more mathematical terms, it's just one damn universe after another. Even so, this would be the end of *our* universe. This is *us*.

The point is not that this is necessarily true but that the very *possibility* of this outcome presents a problem. For classical panentheism, this *should not be possible* because the world is the unfolding of the *necessary* and *inexhaustible* divine being. God cannot possibly run out of energy. The Spirit cannot expire. That would be a metaphysical death of God, which Hegel would say is impossible. There are no conditions under which the unconditional runs out of steam. But as a philosophical-theological discourse, panentheism is in no position to back up its assurances. It all depends upon the mathematics and exper-imental evidence, like what is going around and around in the particle accelerators in Geneva, or what the Webb telescope sights. Panentheists cannot step in and assure the physicists that God is the unconditional and the universe is the body of God, who, as eternal and inexhaustible being-itself, would never stand for the heat death of the universe. That, inciden-tally, was the view actually taken by Lord Kelvin (1824–1907), who proposed the first version of this idea. All panentheism can do is cheerlead, keep its metaphysical fingers crossed, and hope that maybe ours is just one of an infinite multiplicity of endless universes, world without end, amen. That might save God, but it would not save us.

To the theists, this prospect is horrible, and they stand ready to welcome us all back under the big tent of the Supreme Being, like prodigal sons who have learned their lesson the hard way dining among the swine of contingency. Truth to tell, if you have an omnipotent, omniscient Super Somebody in your corner, you can always come up with something. God and the Baltimore Catechism would never stand for it! He had his reasons for letting the *Titanic* perish in the cold Atlantic waters but He would never allow the whole universe to perish. God would just step in and steer our cosmic vessel into safer seas. God could put his divine foot down and say this expansion has gone far enough and command it to stop in its tracks, just as he stopped the sun in its tracks for Joshua (10:12). Of course, the theist's God was the one who started it all, so why not make a universe with no law of entropy or irreversible arrow of time in the first place? Well, that, they say, heads bent back, eyes cast heavenward, in dulcet tones, is a great mystery, which is their most time-tested and no-fail recourse whenever foul winds blow, and they need to go below. God knows what He is doing. Or they could just take the supernaturalist off-ramp: the visible earth and heavens will pass away, and the invisible world will take its place. If you are actually tempted by that line of argument, *stop reading at once*, put a bookmark on this page, and go back to Lesson One. Theism and the supernaturalism with which it usually comes equipped have all the limitations we have been spelling out, and which, if you need reminding, can be reviewed by starting over again. I feel sure you will overcome the temptation and rejoin the argument.

■ ■ ■

Problems and Mysteries. Be assured, I have not just recently arrived on earth after living in a distant galaxy far, far away. I am not denying that there are more urgent problems down here on terra (not so) firma, other matters that matter more than the breakup of matter, more serious issues on our plate than the end of the universe. As problems go, this is not much of a problem. It will take five billion years or so for the sun to die, and by then humanity will have long since disappeared. Anthropogenic climate change overheating the planet is a problem; cosmic heat death is not. Right-wing demagogues spreading dangerous conspiracy theories, undermining the very idea of reason and truth, is a problem; the expansion of the universe is not. Problems are things that provoke people to complain and for which, in principle, at least, there is a solution. But right now no one is complaining about the entropic dissipation of the universe, and when the time comes, there will be no "time" for it to come about in. Talk about scratching where there is no itch!

True, but not the whole truth. While cosmic death is not a *problem*, it is a *mystery.* Problems deal with proximates, while mysteries have to do with ultimates, with matters of ultimate concern, with unconditionals, and what could be more ultimate than the very plausible claim that ultimately it all ends in effective oblivion. I do not mean the mystery of traditional theism, where 𝕲𝖔𝖉'𝖘 ways are mysterious and beyond us, that 𝕲𝖔𝖉 allows the wicked to prosper and the righteous to suffer, and we will never know why. That is to mystify the mystery, to be taken in by the personification. I mean the mystery that is described by radical theology, which is really just thinking radically, which does not fall for the mystification but is no less dissatisfied with rationalistic demystification.

In radical theology, the mystery of why there is something at all rather than nothing is only the half of it; the further mystery is why it will end in oblivion, as seems likely at present. The mystery of being is not only the mystery of to be *or* not to be. It is also the mystery of being rather than nothing at all *and* then eventually nothing at all rather than being. The added mystery is that everything will be forever forgotten, even beyond forgotten, since there will no one around to forget and no one around to remind them, which, for a philosophy of Spirit, is certainly dispiriting. The heat death of the universe is not a problem to be cracked, but it is a mystery to be meditated.

So, the fate of the cosmos merits our attention not because there is anything we can do about it, like remembering to load the lifeboats, but because, if we adopt a cosmic perspective, there is something to *understand*, and if it cannot be understood, then to know how to stand under it, something imponderable to *ponder*, to *interpret* it, to *think*. If your standard of judgment is strictly bottom-line long-term success, in the long run we are all dead. Death succeeds in showing all our successes are short-term. Death makes a mockery of all our lasting cities and long-term plans; it levels every purportedly permanent human accomplishment. Anyone who thinks they can mock death, remove the sting from death, is deceiving themselves. Judged *strictly* in terms of *long-term* outcomes, life really is "a tale told by an idiot, full of sound and fury, signifying nothing," says the Bard. Life is hard and then we die, say the bumper stickers. However it is put, we are all of us returned to the sheer hurly-burly of the elements from which we emerged in the second creation story in Genesis, waiting for us with inexhaustible patience, ready to receive us back into the chaos from which we were drawn. Now add to this the further irony that the same fate awaits the elements themselves, that they are only a little less mortal than us. This is all a long-term tragicomedy of cosmic proportions. The dark joke is on the elements as well. The same verdict without appeal the stars visit upon us is also visited upon the stars themselves. We are, it would seem, all part of a great cosmic stupidity. The stars are not as bright as they think they are.

■ ■ ■

How to Compose a Canticle to Oblivion. So, as the famous American philosopher Oliver Hardy said to his British colleague Stanley Laurel, that's another fine mess you have gotten us into.

What do we do now? Is anybody going to volunteer for the string quartet?

Is that not the role of panentheism, which is a theological vision hailing the cosmic panorama? Is not panentheism the string quartet, our canticle to creation, indeed, the music creation plays on us, the buzz of being itself buzzing us, the song simmering in the things themselves for which panentheism provides the words?

Maybe back in the day panentheism could have played that tune, but times have changed. It was a lot more uplifting then to sing a song to undying cosmic truth and beauty than to the cold dark expanse of nothingness they are predicting now. Where is the *laudato* or *alleluia*, the *jubilate* or the *gaudate*, in oblivion? Panentheism means God in all, not ending up with nothing at all. In panentheism, the Supreme Being vanished into the ground of being, but it was never imagined that being too would vanish, that even with being-itself we have no lasting city.

Panentheism must nowadays face the verdict of the stars, that the being of God is finite and mortal, in sharp contrast with the God of classical theology with whom, on this point, at least, it had stood shoulder to shoulder. If the universe is the body of God, and the history of the universe is the autobiography of God, the last chapter of every biography is death and the body turns to ashes. History turns out to be the story of the increasing *vanishing* or *weakening* of God, of the birth, life, and death of God, from the birth of the stars to their death in cold, dark dissipation. When the expansion is completed, the universe is depleted. The world-spirit itself gives up its spirit on a galactic Golgotha, uttering a cosmic *Eli, Eli, Lema Sabachthani?* The figure of the cross is of cosmic import.

In radical theology, we are seeking not to remove the sting of death, which would be callous and self-deceptive, but to understand death, to stand under it, not stand over it, not attempt—comically, tragicomically—to deny it. Death is neither the enemy, which is what Paul thought, nor a disease to be cured, which is what posthumanists think. Death is intrinsic to life; it is the way life is passed on to new life. Death is the spooky companion of life. In radical theology, the meaning of death is not to be found *after* death but *in* death, in mortal life.

What would that possibly look like? What would it sound like? *It would sound like the string quartet.* But how is that possible? How do we write a canticle to cosmic extinction? Having made the transition from theism to panentheism, have we been left holding the bag of oblivion? That is the turning point in the argument, the pivot, the transition to the second half of the argument.

WHAT IS REALLY GOING ON?

IT IS a venerable and honored practice in philosophy to take a word everybody understands and give it a meaning nobody understands. Invoking the ancient privilege of my craft, let me say that by an *event* I do not mean simply "what happens," which is what everybody understands, but *what is going on in* what happens. Alternately, the event is not merely what happens, but *what is really happening in* what happens. And, however that is determined, that will turn out to be the thing in which we can *really believe*.

This, I hope you understand, or at least have a head start on understanding, because I have flagged these expressions every time I used them and called out their importance. I have all along been feeling about for what is really going on in prayer, or revelation, for what is really happening with Jesus. When people do "religious" things, like sing or pray or engage in rituals, we ask, what are they *really doing*? What do they *really want*? What do they *really believe*? Whatever it is, that is the *event*.

My hypothesis in the present lesson is that *even if* the physicists are right, make that *especially if* they are, especially if it all ends not with a bang but a whimper, then the event is what will be left still standing. The event is what will survive the end of the world. The entropic dissipation of the cosmos is not the end. Well, maybe I am getting carried away. I take that back. It is the end—in the *ontological* sense (= being-talk). Being will be no more. Sad but true enough; I cannot contest that. But that ending is a beginning. That closing is an opening. To what? To still another universe? If I knew that, I would get the Nobel Prize in physics. No, I mean it is an opening to what we are calling the *axiological*, from *axios*, meaning what is genuinely valued *for itself*, not for what you can get with it in return; it is what is held in the highest esteem and prized for its own *intrinsic worth*. Think of an axiom not as a lifeless bit of high school geometry but as a principle whose validity speaks for itself; it will not heed anyone contesting it and does not need anyone offering it further support.

Radical theology is a *theology of events*. That is my axiom, my e=mc², my final answer, my grand finale, after which I bow and leave the stage, hopefully not to supine and somnolent silence but to a standing ovation. That means it is a search for what is really going on in and under the name (of) "God," for what we can really believe in and under this name. In a theology of the event, it is axiomatic that the end of ontology is the beginning of axiology. As a corollary of our axiom, very valuable for ground-diggers, and for life generally, we add, if you have dug yourself into a hole, stop digging. So this axiom must provide us with a lifeline, a ladder, a way to climb out of the cavernous condition in which we seem now to have landed ourselves. For, given the bad news the physicists are delivering, what could possibly be the good news? If the God of theism is an alien power (Lesson Two), and the God of panentheism (Lesson Three) is mortal, if being-itself, the ground of being, is as star-crossed as the rest of us (Lesson Seven), we seem to be in deep trouble (excrementally deep), steeped in questions:

How can God still be what we call *God?*
How can God be unconditional?
What is unconditional about a *mortal God?*
What is so unconditional about the unconditional?
What sort of *future* is left for God? Or for us?
Why not just say life is a tale told by an idiot and be done
    with all this thinking?

So our work is cut out for us. Let's start here with the event itself, any event, and then, in Lessons Nine and Ten, take up the *theology* of the event, and, finally, in Lessons Eleven and Twelve, try to land this ship in an *axiology* of the event.

■ ■ ■

What Is an Event? I begin with a simple example: a trip to the shopping mall in search of a new hat. So we ask, as only a philosopher would (and maybe a Madison Avenue executive or two), what is *really going on* here? We all know that satisfying this desire will not satisfy our "desire" because this particular desire is part of a never-ending chain of ever more desires. Once you find the hat you want, you will then find that you are no longer satisfied with your coat, and then your shoes start looking bad, not to mention that your house needs painting. And on and on. Jean-Paul Sartre said that makes life a useless passion, which cannot be that far from a tale told by an idiot. He really meant that. He *was* awarded the Nobel Prize for saying things like that, and he actually turned it down. Albert Camus said this makes life look like the story of Sisyphus. That also made quite a sensation back in the heyday of existentialism.

For myself, I think Sartre and Camus are complainers. I find desires highly desirable. The ongoing succession of desires makes life interesting, a journey that I, for one, am in no hurry to complete. Desire does not doom us to dissatisfaction. Desires inciting more desires just shows that we are creatures of time, with hopes and expectations. The problem is not that our desires are never fully satisfied; the real problem starts when desiring stops, when desire withers away. That is the sickness unto death, unless we are already dead. The complete cessation of desire is a good working definition of death. When we asked our novice director, who was the very soul of discipling his desires, when temptations against our vow of chastity (sexual desire) will cease, he said, "Fifteen minutes after you are dead." My experience so far is that he was right.

Our very makeup as human beings is to be creatures of desire. To put it ontologically, our very *being* lies in *being-open* to *more being*, to the future, and if the future, then the *possible*. It was in that sense that Heidegger said that possibility is higher than actuality. Then the philosophical question becomes, beyond these particular desires, what do we *really desire*? That is hard to say. Happiness, Aristotle said. True, but that leads to the next question, to heated debates about what will really make us happy, which are also never-ending, not from a lack of answers but from a surplus of too many answers. But whatever we would settle upon—and, truth to tell, there is no one answer—what is *really going on* when we desire this or that belongs to the sphere of the event.

One way to put this is to say we are constituted by an indefinite "desire beyond desire," beyond the desire for this or that, like a new hat, a desire for "something-I-know-not-what." I am not complaining. On the contrary, I take the nonknowing here to be creative not destructive. We are open to a future that Derrida calls an "absolute secret"—"absolute" meaning not only factually unknown but structurally unknowable and undeterminable. So what is *really going on in* all these particular desires is a structure of *expectation*, of openness to what is coming, which inhabits our hopes and desires, disturbing them from within.

Inquietum est cor nostrum, St. Augustine famously said, our hearts are restless. If you know even basic Augustine, you know I am leaving out the rest of this sentence—"and they will not rest until they rest in Thee." I do this on purpose because by that Augustine meant when we are dead. Like most people, I would rather be restlessly alive than resting in peace. I do need my rest, but not that much. I identify the source of this restlessness, and the object of that desire beyond desire, with the event. So, at the risk of sounding excessively cute—another hazard of my occupation—if we ask, "What is the event?," the answer is, "It *is* not, not yet, and we cannot say *what* it is, not yet. The *not yet* is blocking the *what*."

Now let us take a closer look at this situation. When I desire something, it is in effect acting on me already as a lure, which is why the Madison Avenue advertising executives may audit this lesson, and why they design very glittery shopping malls that excite our desires for things we previously did not think we desired. Maybe one of them has been reading Heidegger. As a lure, it is calling to me, and I, for my part, respond. So the event is a call. The call of the event is the event of the call. The call does not *exist*, the call *calls for* existence (there is the "not yet"). By a call I do not mean a telephone ringing, but I also do not mean anything exotic or occult. Apart from the call of the shopping mall, we are all familiar with the "little voice," the "call of conscience," as in *something tells me* not to do that, or the little voice that says this smiling salesman in the shopping mall is lying through his teeth.

The call can even be *silent*, like the reproving look we get back from the face in the mirror when we brush our teeth, which is silently saying, "You know it but you will not say it. You know it but you will not do it." The call is calling but we will not answer. Until we do. If we ever do. But we do not want to go too far with this analogy. Unlike the call of conscience, the call of the event is not merely negative, nagging, and reproving. The event is also—indeed, before all else—profoundly *affirmative*. Remember, I am not a complainer. I am not grumbling about desires. Desire is the desire for more being. I am all for that. Nor is it merely private. Entire communities are organized around a call. All of Judaism is organized around the Shema, Hear, O Israel, a call that constitutes the people as a people, as a people of God. The Statue of Liberty is issuing a call to which a lot of Americans today have covered their ears. In fact, if a community is not gathered in answer to a call, it is just a bunch of people who happen to have the same zip code.

To spell this out a little more, let us say the event is a call

- which calls from the *future*, which is what is being *called for* or promised or desired;
- which calls from the *past*, which is what seeks to be *recalled*, something that has always been simmering in the back of our mind;
- which calls upon us in the *present*, calls for a *response*, calls for action, in the *moment* of decision.

Put all three together (you would never have been able to separate them in the first place), and we can say that the "living present" is not a mere mathematical now-point dividing past and future (Aristotle) but an open space, pried open on both ends by what is being called for and what is being recalled, which calls for action (Heidegger), which is why our hearts are restless (Augustine's *inquietum*). I do not know how much time you have to read the collected works of Aristotle, Augustine, and Heidegger, but that is not the worst one-line summary of all three thinkers at once that I have read.

Again, if we jack this up into the language of ontology, this being (us) whose being lies in the desire of more being, is a being of time, permeated through and through by *temporality*. If you can find the time, Heidegger's most famous book, *Being and Time*, is for my money (I bought several copies, in German and in English) the most important philosophy book written in the twentieth century, and it is a magisterial elaboration of just that point, albeit in somewhat mind-bending prose (the German is crazy, and the English is faithful to the German).

The event is the event of time, the time of the event—not like the tick-tock of clock time, but a "lived time" exposed to the pull of the past and the lure of the future, oscillating in the moment of decision. If being means imperturbable presence, which is what swelled the heart of the ancient Greeks, then the event is time's disturbance of being's peace, making being restless (*inquietum*) with the future and the past, with a promise and a memory, a puzzling commingling of presence-and-absence.

If the Greeks dressed down time as a now-point that cannot hold firm, we return the insult with the comeback that eternity is a frozen, mummified now. The event is what is coming, what is possible (the "not yet"), which recalls the past, which is "already there." We are calling for and being called by a future that will be the future of the past. In our own personal lives, we do not shed our past; like it or not, we fulfill it in unexpected ways (or fail to). That is why I started this book with my life under the eyes of the priests and nuns. My premise is that everybody has some kind of story to tell like that.

So, next up is to look more closely at the temporality of the event.

■ ■ ■

The Future. I start with the future because, while we sometimes want to forget the past or escape the present, we all want to have a future. Indeed, not wanting to have a future, as sometimes happens, signifies serious distress, something seriously amiss in life. We live in time with one eye on the future. Even as you read this book (if you have gotten this far!) you have an implicit idea of what you will do with the rest of the day, and of the week, and of . . . well, you see where that is going. So, in speaking of the time of the event, the future is primary. Even our interest in the past is not mere curiosity; it centers on the possibilities for the future in the past. It is both important and fascinating to study history but if we get lost in the past, Hegel says, we are like bank cashiers, who spend their lives counting other people's money. Just so, we cannot get lost in dreaming of the future because the presence of the past keeps intruding upon and informing our dreams.

The future may mean a future we can anticipate, can see coming, can see is possible. Let us call that the *future present.* The event *in the strict sense*—in the philosophical sense that differs a bit from ordinary usage—is the coming of what we *cannot see coming,* what we will call the *absolute future,* the future for which we cannot be ready, which takes us by surprise; that is what we just called the *absolute secret.* When it comes to events, we have to be prepared to be unprepared. When we desire this or that, this new hat, that takes place within the familiar horizon of everyday life. But the event, what is really going on in this desire, is the coming of something that shatters our horizon of expectation. You set out in search of a new hat and by the time you get home, your whole life has been changed. In that sense, to give it a certain flair, we could say the event is the coming of *the* impossible. I will say more about *the* impossible in the next lesson, but let me say now that I do not mean a contradiction in terms, like a square circle, but a contradiction of our expectations, of what we thought was possible. When events happen, we say, "How was that possible?" "Can you believe that actually happened?" "That was unbelievable!" As such, the event belongs to a hope beyond hope, not for this or that particular thing, but for something, I know not what, let's just say for life itself. This is what sustains us when all seems hopeless, when we "hope against hope," and, if that fails, we fall into despair. So it is beginning to look like what we really believe in is the unbelievable! It is *the* unbelievable in which we really have faith.

Now, there are two important qualifications here. First, I am not mad. I am not suggesting that the future-present, the fore-seeable future of everyday life, is boring and unimportant. Without it, life in time would collapse into chaos; a life of incessant unforeseeable events would be incoherent and traumatic. The future present demands our respect and attention, and it would be irresponsible not to plan for it, like not planning for the education of our children or for our old age or for the due date on our credit cards.

Second, I am not a cockeyed optimist. I am not saying that the event is all good news. You set off to buy a new hat and you may meet the love of your life standing in line in front of you, *or* you may have a terrible life-changing accident. The good news would be an event (making all things new), but the event is not necessarily good news (it could make all things new by making everything worse). Events are what happen when you had other plans. The event is the unforeseeability lodged *within* the future-present, say, on the way to the shopping mall, the unforeseeability embedded *in* the foreseeable future, which *inhabits* the future-present and disturbs it *from within*. Our heart is *restless*, which means both *expectant* of the future (promise), and also *uneasy* about it (threat). Instead of luring us the future may very well loom over us. So the event is a *promise/ threat*, the repository of both our deepest fears *and* our highest hope, and not one without the other. If we try to be excessively safe, cautious to a fault, we narrow our future and reduce our chance for something renewing. That could be the love of our life standing in front of us in line, but not if we don't open our mouths. Eliminate all risk and we risk having life pass us by. *By* the event, *by* the impossible, *by* the unbelievable, everything new comes about, but that is risky business.

■ ■ ■

The Event Is the To-Come. To see the next point, it would help to raise our level of expectation to something bigger and more important than a new hat, like our desire for democracy, which, we know, is a fragile thing. The *existing* democracies are at best a promissory note of the democracy we *desire*, let's say, the *democracy-to-come*. So, in speaking of events, all the nouns come attached with a coefficient of the infinitival, not the infinite but the infinitive *to-come*.

Then does that not mean that the event of the democracy-to-come *is* an essence or what-ness after all, an *ideal essence*? Is it not a Platonic Form, a Kantian Ideal, of Democracy, in caps, a limit-concept, which we are striving to reach one step at a time? Not so, but that is exactly the right question to raise, which is why I brought it up. The *ideal* future is not the absolute future but the future present. Why? Because we have an "idea" of what we want, and we can see whether it is being gradually realized, asymptotically approached—like losing ten pounds to hit our ideal BMI. The mark of the future-present is that I can see what I desire, and I can see that it is just not here yet.

But the event *going on in* the name (of) "democracy" is an *absolute* future, an absolute *secret*, an *unforeseeable* and *nonessential open-endedness*. Then what business do we have calling it democracy? How do we know what to call it? Another excellent question. We do not. What is to-come, what we *really desire* when we desire democracy, what we are dreaming of, *what is going on in* the word *democracy*, *may not* bear that name at all, if or when it comes. So let us say that, at best, its least bad name is what we at present call *democracy*. In speaking of the democracy-to-come, the *to-come* (*à-venir*), which is the event (*événement*), is more important than the "democracy," which is an historical construction, a conditional name for the undeconstructible (Derrida), a Vorstellung (Hegel), a symbol (Tillich), a theopoetic figure (radical theology)—of something *unconditional*. The event is something of which we dream, not an idle daydream but an urgent Martin Luther King Jr. dream, for which we are willing to put ourselves (not others) in harm's way, to put everything at risk.

The event is not some stable essence or presence or whatness, like Democracy, enshrined in big stone buildings and monuments, but a wisp of a thing, like a ghost, a dream of the open-ended process of something coming whose point of departure—we begin where we are—is today called *democracy*. We affirm democracy by *hyper*affirming it, affirming to the point of *excess*. Let us say we love it to pieces! That is, we allow it to overflow, to exceed itself, to release the event it harbors.

■ ■ ■

The Past. Now let us consider the *past* of the event. When we are asked to put things in our own words, they are never actually our own; they are the words we learned in the world that was already up and running when we first opened our mouths. Our word *democracy* is not *our* word. *Democracy* is an old Greek word handed down to us, like almost all our words, by our history. If we were born somewhere else or in another time, we might never have heard of it. So, even when we think we are thinking about the future, not the past, the past is nonetheless making its presence felt. The *call* for a democracy-to-come *recalls* a history. This word has a history, or, rather, it *is* the history that has been handed down across countless ages, stretching all the way back to the Greeks, where it emerged from an antecedent history, from the dreams of forgotten people the Greeks never heard of, from time immemorial, from a past that was never present. We are thinking of the future of the past we inherited. The past is not something done and over with. The past is not a graveyard. It is a keyboard waiting for us to start playing, sometimes a golden oldie but even better to improvise and come up with something new. The past is a depository of possibilities for the future in the present.

So, the event is also the *absolute past*, not merely the past-present in the history books but the past that was *never present*, a past from time immemorial. Again, this is nothing occult or exotic. We experience the absolute past in the familiar phenomenon of *nostalgia*. Nostalgia (like everything else) is an iffy proposition, a two-edged sword. Just like the future, the past also poses a promise/threat. Nostalgia is too often a dangerous and reactionary sentiment, dripping with the resentment of reactionaries against a pluralistic future and with their self-deception about a past that never was. Right-wing Christians think the Founders were a bunch of Bible-thumping fundamentalists, not deists who took a pair of scissors to the miracles in the New Testament! But nostalgia can also have an open-ended, creative, welcoming, and generous sense, where we remember a time which *we very well know* never was. We have no illusions; we are not kidding ourselves. We are recalling what is *calling* in the past, remembering a past of which we are dreaming with a Birmingham jail dream, dreaming of the time when all of God's children (not just white land-owning men) will be free. Our memories are what the liberation theologians call "dangerous memories," a danger to our complacency, a danger to the powers that be. We *remember* the *future* of the *past*, the possibilities the past *promised*, what *could have been*, what it still could be, in the subjunctive, if only there were "democracy." You could say we are remembering the future! Or trying to get back to the future.

■ ■ ■

The Caller of the Call. Finally, the call calls to *us* in the present and calls to *action*, calls for a *response*, which raises the question of just who is calling. Common sense dictates that the call must have a caller. Good point. But common sense also says the earth is flat and immobile, an idea that proved hard to budge. So we must not, as do the bridge-builders, jump to the conclusion that there is an *identifiable* caller in the sense of a particular *somebody* doing the calling. Remember, the unconditional is not Somebody. If we asked the Spirit of the Age to please rise, everyone would keep their seat. Just so with the caller of the call. The Somebody is a personification, a dramatization, of the call, a helpful way of imagining a call that is *getting itself called*—google the "middle voice" in grammar—in all those stories that have been handed down to us. The call is something like an emergent property, which cannot be traced back, one to one, to a singular causal agent, but arises as an effect of a network or a system. It emerges from a collective of countless prophets and mystics, painters and poets, philosophers and scientists, raconteurs and rhapsodes, some namable but most entirely forgotten, not to mention what collectively emerges in ordinary language, which contains deep deposits of our imagination. The call is lodged in stories told by unidentifiable, anonymous, and entangled voices, verbally transmitted and written down, in authentic texts and corrupt ones, from interwoven sources and redacted resources, all but forgotten languages, forged with imperceptible slowness by long forgotten generations—which it is up to *us* to *read*. That means we must not simply respond, but we must assume responsibility for our response and decide what is being called. We do not hear a call and just start marching, which is a familiar way to avoid responsibility ("Just following orders"). We must discern or *interpret* what is being called for (Lesson Three).

That is the event.

Lesson Nine

WHAT IS GOING ON IN THE NAME OF GOD?

NOTICE THAT, with the introduction of the event, the plot has thickened. Now we see that our lives are bordered by two impassable horizons, not only by the unprethinkable facticity of the past but also by the unforeseeability of the future. We find ourselves situated between a past that was never present, coming to us from a time out of mind, and a future we cannot see coming. We live in the space between the unprethinkable and the unforeseeable, touched by their action on us from a distance, slightly spooked by a call we are not sure we heard. That in which we live and move and have our being has now taken on a dual density. Up to now it has gone under the name of being-itself, and the unconditional has meant unconditional facticity of being, which puts a check on thinking. But now we see emerging another side, which is less being than possibility, less *être* than *peut-être*, and the unconditional looks more like a hope.

And hope brings us to God.

In a *theology* of the event, the event we seek travels under the name (of) "God," so the question is, what is really going on, what can we really believe, what do we really desire *in and under the name (of) "God"?* In what can we *hope* in and under this name? The question of God was presented to me on the first page of the Catechism. *"Who is God?"* it asks, and, without worrying itself half to death about the "who" and the "is," not to mention the "God," back comes the reply: "God is the Creator of heaven and earth, and of all things." *Deus omnipotens*, the *mysterium tremendum et fascinans*, which is Latin for the mystery that makes our knees knock before they bend in awe, that makes them bend because they knock (loosely translated). That got my unbroken attention. Think of a storm at sea, with fifty-foot waves, rolling across the waters and landing in southwest Philadelphia, leaving us all awash with awe (brainwashed, some of my old friends say), soaked in trepidation, 𝖌𝖔𝖉, bathed in Christian Gothic Latin or even in plain English, sans serif.

There is an event in there somewhere, but exactly where? Up to now we have said it has to do with the implacable givenness of unprethinkable being. Now we find ourselves lured by the quiet power of the possible.

Ever since I started stargazing as a child, lying on my back and looking up at the sky on summer nights, I wondered if this heavenly vault is a tribute to the majesty of God, as the priests and nuns assured us, or whether, God forbid, nobody knows we are here. This question, "Who is God?," has simmered within me all my life, always waiting for me around the next corner. *Quaestio mihi magna factus sum*, Augustine said. I have become a great question to myself. Have I ever! I did not come up with this question. It came up with me. God and I are in this together, in question together, both of us, spinning together in spooky tandem. Who is God? Who do I want to be? What do I really believe? In what can I hope?

So now we have come to the moment of truth in this little book (which is not to say that there is nothing true in which we have said up to now). What is the *event* harbored in the name (of) "God"? Basically the Baltimore Catechism question, slightly different spin, which might have raised an episcopal eyebrow back in old Baltimore.

■ ■ ■

The Possibility of the Impossible. In Lesson Eight we examined the to-come, the *open-endedness* of the future, of an unconditional promise (which goes along with the threat). The promise of what? Of something-I-know-not-what. That sounds like an evasion, a nonanswer, cloudy confusion, an airy abstraction floating about freely in metaphysical outer space. Not a bit. The nonanswer is made in the affirmative, resolutely keeping the question open. It is the open-endedness embedded *in* the most concrete and on-the-ground desires, like a trip to the shopping mall, whose pockets we search for a desire they conceal, which is the thing which makes us ever restless. Keeping the future open keeps the possibility of the event alive.

Now let us give this a nudge. If a desire, why not dare call it also a *prayer*? Remember, daring to think radically dares to ask questions without fear of hitting theological ground (Lesson One). Contrary to public opinion, if there is one, we radical theologians also pray (Lesson Four), not exactly churchy candle and incense prayers, but a prayer in a perfectly serious sense, nonetheless. If I desire something to-come I am implicitly praying, "Come." If we give up praying in this sense, if we lose our (ontological) faith, if we stop saying, "Come," the spark of the event has flared out, and it is time to put the funeral director's number on speed dial.

In radical theology, "Come" is our first, last, and constant prayer, the prayer *of* the event, the prayer *for* the event, the prayer elicited *by* the event. By *any* event, but *above all* by the name (of) "God," the name to which, in a theology of the event, we attach *paradigmatic* status. There are *other* paradigms, and, depending on where you come from, you might not talk like this at all. But this is the event under excavation here—"God," in caps and in the singular, a common noun become a proper name, belonging to an identifiable complex of historically Abrahamic traditions—which swept across the epochs and landed in my lap before I knew what hit me.

Those of *us* who inherit this tradition can say that whenever I desire this or that I am implicitly *desiring God*. Stated thus, this is twenty-four-karat Augustinianism, the soul of orthodoxy, nothing radical about it. If I said no more I could probably get an imprimatur for this book from the chancellery office downtown. But, not stopping there, I risk the ire of the higher-ups by giving it a different twist, reformulating it in terms of a desire for *the event that is harbored* in the name (of) "God," which elicits episcopal alarm that something illicit is afoot.

Why *paradigmatic?* Because when we say, "May your kingdom come," the "kingdom-to-come" is not just an example of the event; it is *exemplary.* It is the *model* for this whole idea of the event and, I would wager, its very source. Try finding Socrates saying that. The Greeks valorized being over becoming, necessity over contingency, unchanging essence and presence over coming and going, fate over freedom, and their desire, their eros, was to "recollect" what has always already and necessarily been there. True being was always behind them, like something lost. But the event is always ahead. May the kingdom *come,* may it come *true,* may it *happen*—that is the *prophetic* passion, the *messianic* motif, the prophetico-messianic *hope* to "make all things new," resounding in the biblical traditions, going back to Isaiah and the prophets and the early Christian expectation of the second coming.

The call of the to-come, as an opening on to the future, is focused on the *possible,* on what could or may come, not exactly *être,* being, but *peut-être,* may-being, perhaps. Now if among all the omni names of God in classical theology we were to single out one for special honors in radical theology, one that is especially suggestive in a theology of the event, the laurels would go not to being-itself (*ipsum esse*)—the preferred language of Aquinas and Tillich—but to may-being-itself, possibility-itself (*posse ipsum*), which is how it was put forward by a very forward-looking Renaissance theologian named Nicholas of Cusa (1401–1464). For Cusa, God is infinite, uncontainable possibilizing, the deepest repository of possibilities, of which any "actual" thing is a "contraction."

The next step is this. The highest possibility, the possibility we desire above all else—hence the event in the paradigmatic sense—is the possibility of *the* impossible. That is the key. Highlight this: the "possibility of the impossible" is central to what we mean *both* by the *event* (Lesson Eight) and by *God*. The latter point is not a quirk of Derrida but the considered opinion of Matthew (19:26) and Luke (1:37): some things are beyond us mortals, but "for God all things are possible." Whatever is not possible for us is possible for God.

So now we can say that the name of God is the name of a *call* that calls for the coming of *the* impossible, for the possibility of the impossible, to which *we* should be the response. The name of God is a placeholder for the open-endedness of *the* impossible, for a desire that I cannot contract to desiring this or that, for a faith exceeding any belief, for a hope against hope, for a love that is without measure. It stands in for an excess, for a passage to the limits, for an infinitival hope or expectation. The mystery of God springs from the dual mystery of the absolute secret, of the concealed depths, of the unconditional, of the unprethinkable, which outstrips us, which has called upon us before we know what to call it, when we were little more than wombish waterlings, and of an unforeseeable future, when what lies before is, well, God knows what.

Hold on. Have we not landed ourselves right back in the Baltimore Catechism, in the *Deus omnipotens*, the classical notion of omnipotence, of Almighty God, 𝔊𝔬𝔡, who has the power to do anything, like part the seas for the Israelites? Sounds like it, but not quite. The *event* that is going on in the name of God is not *omnipotence* but *omnipotentiality*, the reiteration (radicalization) of omnipotence *as* omnipotentiality, where God is not the God of eternal being but the God of futural *may*-being. In a theology of the event, the *vita ventura* does not mean eternal life; it means the life-to-come. In a theology of the event, the name (of) "God" is a *focus imaginarius* in which everything we love and desire and hope for converge, holding up for us everything we hope may be possible, *however impossible*. Making it actual is up to us.

If I have not backtracked to classical omnipotence in speaking of *the* impossible, neither have I lost all touch with reality. As I said in Lesson Eight, I am not speaking of a logical impossibility, a contradiction in terms (a square circle), but something *experiential*, something that shatters our horizon of expectation, what we dared not dream or hope for, overturning what we thought was possible—in science or art or everyday life—leaving us to wonder how it was possible. *The* impossible is being imaginatively figured (theology as theo*poetics*) in the *stories* of the God who populated the barren land and sea and sky with living things, stopped the sun in its tracks for Joshua (10:12–14), and made a virgin womb fertile—marvelous metaphors all, famous and fetching figures of a theopoetic imagination (Lesson Six). Literalizing these stories kills the spirit, prevents the event, dispirits the aspiration, calls down on them the disdain of the cultured despisers, which is religion making itself unbelievable. These scenes dance on the edge of our imagination, turning precarious pirouettes on the margins of *the* un/believable, *the* impossible, imaginative figurations of a hope beyond hope, a desire beyond desire, like those times when we face an "impossible" situation "hoping for a miracle." What we really believe in is the *un*believable, for which the name of God does service.

The *exemplary* example of this is the New Testament itself, where *the* impossible takes the striking form not of a square circle but of a scandal and a stumbling block, the topsy-turvy scene of the kingdom of God. The word *kingdom* (*basileia, regnum*) has fallen on bad times, poor thing, because it resounds with royalty and authoritarianism, power and patriarchy, even theocracy. But here it refers to a world that has reversed our expectations, where offense is met with forgiveness, the first are last and the last are first, the poor are privileged and the rich have a very narrow needle to thread, and we are asked to love our enemies, all of which is pretty well-nigh impossible. All the expected effects of power, authority, and hierarchical rule are *reversed*, resulting in the rule of the unruly, the reign of the unroyal, a hier*an*archy, a "sacred anarchy," as I like to say. This kingdom of ill-born and powerless people (1 Cor. 1:26) looks mad to the "world," to Aristotle's man of practical wisdom, a good-looking and well-educated aristocratic chap, and nothing like a real man to a heartless Roman warrior. This is a "kingdom" in an ironic sense, actually mocking the authoritarianism and patriarchy. The possibility of *the* impossible is neither theological (omnipotence) nor logical (a contradiction in terms) but theopoetic, a kind of theopoetic cardiology, the heart of a heartless world.

■ ■ ■

But How Can God Still Be God? Now back to the hard question raised in Lesson Eight. In a theology of the event, how could God still be *unconditional*? If the Supreme Being is an imaginative personification of the ground of being, and if the ground of being is vanishing (Lesson Seven), if the stars are mortal, if God is as star-crossed as the stars themselves, what is left? Why are we even talking about God? How can God still be what we call *God*?

As we learn from our political leaders, the best way to answer a tough question is to change the subject! Answer the question you would rather answer. So, if we are pressed, *ontologically*, how something without power can be *unconditional*, the answer is, *axiologically*. Panentheism, for example, is *pen*ultimately right, not as an ontology but as an axiology, not as a *proposition* but as a *prayer*. Panentheism is right, not in the indicative, that God *is* all in all, but in the optative, that God *may be* all in all, that God *may* prove to be that in which we live and move and have our being. That is our *hope!* That is what we hope and pray and desire, but that is a test God must pass, and God depends on us, so it is a test we both must pass. The event takes place in the optative, which is the voice of hope.

Stop thinking of God ontologically, as an *agent*, and start thinking axiologically, where the Spirit is an aspiration. God is not an independent agent-doer of mighty deeds, who does things for us, like save us from our enemies, clear all the plastic bottles out of the ocean, and put a halt to carbon emissions, just so long as we pray hard enough and give up our favorite treats for Lent. If that is how you think of God, then you should give up God for Lent. The *agency* is *our* responsibility. The name of

God is not found in the nominative, but in the invocative (and provocative)—that something may be done, which may or may not happen, depending on us, so we are in the accusative.

The name (of) "God" is not the name of a being up there (theology), nor of the ground of being down here (onto-theology) but of a *call* for being (axiology) to which *we* should be the response (theopraxis). The name of God is not the name of a being who is going to reward us just so long as we behave ourselves but who is coming to get us on Judgment Day if we misbehave. When I was a child, I spoke as a child, but now I know that would ruin everything. I am not dismissing the "fear of God," but demystifying it, depriving it of its Gothic cloud of confusion and powers of intimidation. *Fear* is not a bad word. It is meant to keep us safe, but, as St. Augustine said, we must distinguish a "servile fear," like the fear of being punished by an omniscient, omnipotent Super-being, from a "chaste fear," let us say love's fear, the fear that we will stop loving, or love unwisely, the fear that we will make ourselves unworthy of what is happening to us, which is the fear we nourish and cherish in radical theology (Lesson Eleven).

The final step in radical theology is to effect the axiological shift, to relocate the name of God from the ontological to the axiological order, from the order of being to the order of maybeing. That means that the name of God is the name of a call that calls *unconditionally but without power.* The call calls but it does not come bearing arms. It has laid down its sword.

Let me be clear. This is neither sour grapes nor infinite resignation. I am not saying that it would be a lot better if the call did have being and power but, as it does not, we just have to play with the hand we are dealt. On the contrary, I am arguing that the unconditional, *as such*, if there is such a thing, is *only possible* without power. Not only *can* it be, but it *can only be* unconditional without power. The event is unconditional not *in spite of* but *because* it is not backed up by the power of being, not endowed with the prestige of presence, but left defenseless, trembling like a leaf in the winds of im/possibility. Once the unconditional comes bearing a sword, its unconditionality is compromised. Remember Constantine, when the persecuted church became the persecutor, and a church once pacifist began defending "just war" theory, colluding with the powers of this world, exposing the bipolar makeup of theology, preaching peace and powerlessness as a way of insinuating itself into a position of worldly power. If Jesus ever said, "Blessed are those who wage a just war," we have lost the manuscript. The only way for the unconditional to have power is to have it as if it had it not (*hos me, quasi non*).

■ ■ ■

The Weakness of God. In order to keep the theology of the event, of call and response, safe from omnipotence and imperialism, I characterize it as "weak theology." I am not advocating spinelessness and indecision but stressing that the name of God is the name of a *call* where the call itself, of itself, if it had a self, is a weak force. I am not against being, power, and strength. I am saying the *strength* is supplied by the *response*, which is on us. The call is weak. Think of how easily and regularly the call of conscience is ignored, or how the Sermon on the Mount, one of the most subversive and explosive—impossible—texts in Western history, is also one of the most compromised (Richard Holloway). So *we* have to be strong. The call *as such* calls, but without an army to enforce what it is calling for. In the "world," it is not what God is calling for that calls the shots but the big shots, what the New Testament calls the "powers and the principalities," the big money, the big institutions, like the state or the market, which include, please note, religion, the church and the university—basically, the people who write the paychecks.

The call of "justice" is a weak force that calls without real power, but if the police pay you a call, you are in real trouble, justly or not. If you are on the wrong side of justice, you may still walk the streets with impunity, but if you are on the wrong side of the law, you are behind bars, justly or not. Justice itself, of itself, calls without what they call in the gangster films an *enforcer*, a strong arm, a Supreme Being on high to issue threats, or even the ontological support of the ground of being to sustain it from down below.

The lesson of history is that the powers that *be* are stronger than the call for what *may be*. Our history bears sorry witness against us. As James Kugel said, the history of God actually intervening on behalf of the persecuted and staying the hand of the wicked is so bad you have to wonder why the theologians keep bringing it up. Or, as the great theologian of "Black liberation" James Cone said, if the death of Jesus on the cross made us all free, conquered Satan, and dispersed his minions, somebody should tell the white people.

■ ■ ■

The Dangerous Perhaps. Another way to put this point is to say that the classical theology of the Supreme Being is a theology of the *supreme good*. Weak theology is not a theology of the good; it is a theology of the *event*, which is supremely risky. It is a theology of what Nietzsche (another atheist from whom theology stands to learn a thing or two) called the "dangerous perhaps," for the event is a promise/threat, a possibility to be actualized—for better or for worse. The name of God is the name of an *excess*, meaning it is what the world *would look like*, in the subjunctive, if justice flowed like water over the land, unless it is the name of the *worst* excesses, our best alibi for watering the killing fields with rivers of innocent blood. When we take the name of God in vain, all hell breaks loose. God is a consuming fire (Heb. 12:29), which also means God is the best way to burn the whole place down. As Jack Miles says, God is not a saint. God is a risk. I would hazard the guess that more people have been killed in the name of God than of any other name, except maybe justice or love or the fatherland. Someone should do a survey. *Pro deo et patria*, which was the motto of the Christian Brothers high school I attended, can make for a lethal combination.

The name of God trembles with what Heidegger call the "quiet power of the possible," but that is also the *peril* of the possible, so it stands in permanent need of interpretation, of wise discernment (hermeneutics). The name (of) "God" does not get a pass; it is not a magic wand. It will not keep us safe; we have to keep it safe. When we speak of a Messiah, recognize that *we* are the messianic age (Walter Benjamin). *We* are the ones the dead are waiting for to make right the wrongs that were done to them—not some mystical magus coming over the hill on a white horse with a sword in his mouth to slay the nations (Rev. 19:11–16).

I am not trying to transfer God's omnipotence to us. I do not think anything is omnipotent, God or us. I am maximizing not our power, which is clearly limited, but our responsibility, which is unlimited, which calls for courage, not only the courage to be but also the courage for what may be, the courage to hope. The name of God is a call to assume responsibility for ourselves, as Bonhoeffer says.

I am also not engaged in a blanket condemnation of power. I am saying that the unconditional is without power, but *we* are not. We are asked to supply the power. There are people in high office with real power who have the strength of character to *respond* to the powerless power of the unconditional in exercising their power. Religious leaders like Pope Francis or Bishop Tutu could use the power of their office to serve themselves but they choose instead to serve the servants of God. Just so, there are public servants (an endangered species) in high political office who prioritize serving the people or the planet over serving their party and their own personal interests. The deconstruction of power does not destroy power; it divides, redistributes and multiplies it. Everyone who suffers from oppression needs and deserves to have the power to stand up to their oppressors. To deconstruct power is not to decimate power but to disseminate it so as to insure it lifts up the lowliest instead of holding them down. Weak theology is simply dispelling the illusion that some supernatural power is going to come to our rescue, simply saying that the name of God is the name of an event, of a dream for which we are to provide the reality, of a promise on which we are expected to make good. We are expected to make ourselves part of the history of God, of what is going on in and under the name (of) "God." We are expected to be part of the history of hope.

Lesson Ten

WHETHER GOD WILL HAVE BEEN

IN A theology of the call, something is missing in God—
namely, the *response*; namely, the *world*; namely, *us*. *God needs
us.* The name of God pays its own way, proves its own truth,
validates itself in a history that proves itself worthy of the name
of God—or *does not*—and, for that, God help us, God depends
upon us. So the consequence of the *axiological* shift we made in
Lesson Nine is that the question of God is not exactly "Does
God exist?" but whether God *will have been.* The existence of
God turns out to be the entangled existence of God-with-us,
Emmanuel. God's existence, like ours, is contingent, fragile,
unstable, and uncertain, because it is dependent upon the extent
to which *we* manage to make this event come true. If the *insistence* of the event that is harbored in the name of God is called
the *prius*, then the *existence* of God will be determined after the
fact, a posteriori. Only time will tell, and time is history, and
history is not over until it is over. When we pray "come" for the

coming of the kingdom, nobody is coming to save us. The coming kingdom is waiting to see if we come through. Nothing guarantees that we will. The name of God is not the name of being up there or out there but of a form of life down here; it is not the name of eternal being but temporal may-being. What is going on in that name is enacted, actualized—unless it is not, of course—in people who make it real, make it happen, the people who make the "kingdom" come true, who bring it about in people's lives, down here on the ground, in obscure pockets of the world, in dirt-poor church halls and third-world health clinics serving the poorest of the poor.

■ ■ ■

The Entanglement of God and Me. As opposed to classical theology, we and God are entangled like a pair of particles in quantum physics. God's call calling and our responding are like two particles spinning in the same field, or, more simply, two sides of the same coin. God's being is not *necessary* but *needy*, in need of our response. This is a scene of mutual entanglement, of unsettled turmoil in me reflecting the unsettled state of affairs in God—unless it is the opposite.

God is not a *plenitude* who empties the divine being into the world, who dies into the world, which is the Nietzschean spin the "death of God" theologians put on Paul (Phil. 2:7), but an *emptiness* seeking fulfillment in the world, who comes to life in the world. There (here) God hopes to find life, existence and reality, a place to stretch the divine limbs and relieve the divine loneliness. God's relationship to the world is not *kenotic* (death of God) but *pleromatic* (life of God). Without the world, God would be left in the lonely isolation of the opening line of Genesis, surveying a barren void without the companionship of living things, the divine call unanswered, the divine dreams unfulfilled, more lonely than the solitary self-thinking thought of Aristotle, who appears to be eternally satisfied with himself and unmindful of us.

Accordingly, in posing the question of God, the questioners are drawn into the question, their future put into question, and who they really are is on the line. The question "Who is God?" recoils into a series of further questions: "Who is asking—and what do you desire? Who do you want to be? What do you really believe? In what do you hope?" Tell me what you desire and I will tell you who you are and who your God is, who *God* will have been. What I make of God and what I make of myself run in tandem. The measure I take of God is the measure I make of me. The event by which I become myself and the event by which God becomes God are the same. We are two possibilities actualized by the same act. We sync up—for better or for worse. So much God, so much self, which is good Augustinianism, and conversely, which is the radical twist. What is going on in the name of God pushes me to the limits.

Who am I? I am the one who wants to know, who desires to know what I desire, what I truly desire and really believe. I am the one who is wary of saying "I." Who am I? You tell me. How can I say? To be sure, I have an identity card, several of them, which I can use to board an airplane. But if the airline attendant were of a philosophical frame of mind and pressed me for my true identity, who *in truth* I truly am, who I *really* am, and what I *really* believe, I would be thrown into profound confusion and consternation. I would make a spectacle of myself, bursting into tears, confessing with St. Augustine that I am a land of difficulty and turmoil. I have an identity, but I am not identical with myself. There are too many things going on in me, too many voices, roles, relationships, desires. It is too much for me to say I *am* such and such, all the way down, this and only this, through and through. Were someone to make a recording of all these voices inside me, I would not be able to identify who was saying what to whom.

When I say "I" I am hoping I can get away with it. Who am I? The question is the answer. This "I" is a grammatical fiction I use to get myself onto airplanes. I am multitudes (Walt Whitman), which makes polytheism look like the theology of choice (Lyotard). I multiply daily. It depends on who is asking and what day they ask me. Who I am I do not. What I do I am not. I am of several minds, spirits, specters, possessed by many muses, too many—theistic and atheistic, polytheistic and panentheistic, religious and anti-religious, poetic and scientific, loyal and unfaithful, a loner and a communitarian, wise and foolish—and they give me no rest.

This is all just a way of saying I am not dead yet. When I am dead you can say, as I cannot, who I *will have been*. Then my restless heart will rest in peace. Events are for life, essences are for eulogies on the late lamented, pious pronouncements over the dearly departed, who had his faults but we all sorely miss. The source of all that trouble in me is the *event*, the *truth* of the event, the possibility of the impossible, and the trouble spreads like wildfire, racing up and down the hills and canyons of my life, spanning the length and breadth of my being, of all being, up to the Supreme Being and down to the ground of being, both the supreme and the supine, up and down, all around, superficial and profound, including God.

Especially God. This goes for God as much as it does for me, for us!

■ ■ ■

Whether God Will Have Been—the Onus Is on Us. The hook I used at the start to get your attention was to say that, in radical theology, to the question "Does God exist?" the right religious and theological reply is, "Atheism." Adieu to God. May God rid us of 𝕲𝖔𝖉 (Eckhart).

But if we put this question *again*, if we demystify and reiterate it, this time in terms of the partnership of God and us, in terms of the call of the *event* going on the name (of) "God" to which *we* are supposed to be the response, we get a different answer. Now if we ask, safely removed beyond the reach of ecclesiastical supervision and interdiction, "Does the God of the event exist?," the right religious and theological reply is, "*We do not know yet.*" If the name of God is the *insistence* of a call, then the *existence* of God is *what God will have been*, when they write the history of the response, which is the history of *us*, and history is not over yet. God's *essence* is in our hands. We can only speak in terms of what the grammarians call the *future perfect*, which does not insure a perfect future but describes the future that will have happened, which may be quite imperfect.

Theology is theo*praxis*. The meaning of the name of God is the form of life in which it issues. We are the practice of God in the world, God at-work (*en-ergeia*) in the world, the enactment of God in the world, our lives having been set in motion by what is going on in this name. If God is infinite possibility, the burden of actualization falls on us. The name of God is the name of something to do, a deed, a task, and the task is to make ourselves worthy (*axios*, worth, value) of what is going on in the name of God, which is to say, to make ourselves part of the history of God. The question is really not "What does this name 'mean'?," as if it were a puzzle to be solved, but, like a musical score or a dramatic script, "How do we play it?"

Theology is not like a dead language—not for lack of trying on the part of some theologians!—where we can be sure that there will be no more speakers, no more poets, no more metaphors or mutations, where we can collect every usage and definitively inventory what a given word meant. In a dead language, we are certain there will be no events. It was a cunning move on the part of orthodoxy to induce that illusion, to put everything to sleep with the dormitive power of Latin and then to lace up the Latin in funereal Gothic garments! The immutability of God was insured by being interred in a no less immutable dead language. Who would dare to differ with 𝔇𝔢𝔲𝔰? Just you dare!

Radical theology is for the living, where the future is still to-come, which is as true for God as it for us. It is up to us to make ourselves worthy of what is going on in that name—and that, as we say, "remains to be seen." God includes the unforeseeable remainder. The "existence of God" is not established by a logical argument but *testified to* in the time and trouble, the tests and tempests of existence, in the testimony given in the history of what goes on in and under the name (of) "God." "See how they love one another"—or see how they don't! That is the history of *us*, in the *accusative*—*me voici*, which literally means see me here, I showed up! In an axiology, showing God's existence depends on whether we show up.

In those terms, the strongest argument for the existence of God is the people in the working church, the people in the trenches, the lives of people selflessly serving the least among us, testifying to the subversive power of the Sermon on the Mount, the people who answer to the Spirit, not their superiors. Just so, the strongest argument against it is a wave of white supremacists, truth deniers, theme park theologians, of sexual abusers and clerical cover-ups, a patriarchal hierarchy, all of whom are giving the name of God a bad name, making God ashamed of being God, who are going to shame God right out of existence. The name of God is the name of the best in us and the worst. It is not identical with itself; it is a bit bipolar, just like us.

If God were a great star, it would be of a highly unusual sort, one that needs us to shine upon and feel its warmth. We are entangled with God, spinning together in a spooky tandem with God. We are both in this together. In what? In the soup of existence, in responding to the call of the kingdom-to-come, in making the kingdom come true. The event has no army to carry out its orders, no papers to establish its credentials, no headquarters or central offices downtown, no powerful computers or 3D printers. The sole testimony to the existence of the call is the response, so answering the call looks foolish to the world, like dancing to music no one else can hear.

The future of God is not just epistemological uncertainty; it is ontological indeterminacy. It has not happened yet. It depends on what will have been.

The weakness of God is that God does not exist; God insists. The folly of God is that God leaves existence up to us.

MAKING OURSELVES WORTHY OF WHAT IS HAPPENING TO US

IN AN axiology, everything comes down to love. If you want to know what you really believe, ask yourself what you really love. Really believing is not a matter of doctrines and propositions but of love. We do not put our love where our belief is; we put our believing where our love is. We do not love because we believe; we believe because we love. It is far better to believe in what we love than to be in love with what we believe. So now the question is, *what* do we love? What do we *really* love? Is it *worthy* of us? Is it *worthy of God*, who is love? Are we making ourselves worthy of what we love, of what is going on in the name (of) "God"—whether or not we believe in God? Are not the worst things done in the name of love? That is the question. Might it also be the answer?

■ ■ ■

God Is Love. We can do no better than to take our lead here from the question Augustine raised in his *Confessions*: "What do I love when I love you, my God?" We also can do no better than to do so by means of the fascinating way it is taken up by Jacques Derrida in his *Circumfession.* Derrida puts himself in Augustine's shoes or kneels down beside him on his prie-dieu and *reenacts* Augustine's prayer, *repeating* it for himself. That speaks volumes about what he called "deconstruction." Instead of launching a reductionistic rationalist critique or an atheistic attack from without, instead of hammering Augustine for his Neoplatonic dualism, which is the old Enlightenment, Derrida situates himself within the *Confessions* and assumes Augustine's prayerful posture, feeling around for the event, for what is really going on in the name of "loving God"—even though Derrida "rightly passes for an atheist"—which is the new Enlightenment.

The *circum* in this title signifies, among other things, the cut of his Judaism—well, of his memory of Judaism, what remains of the Judaism in which he was born and raised in colonial Algeria, making him a "compatriot" of Augustine (modern Algeria is ancient Numidia). This "nostalgeria," as he calls it, still lingers somewhere in his heart, now in his fifty-ninth year as his mother lies dying in Nice, like Monica in Ostia. His readers knew about Derrida's atheism, everyone knew except his mother, who would ask others if "Jackie" (his birth name, which we share!) still believed in God, he the "son of her tears." But Derrida surprised us all in this text by saying that he has been asking himself Augustine's question all his life, translating it into his own life, so that the emphasis falls on the "my," what I love when I love *my* God. The name of God is the name of his love, of his desire, of his faith in impossible things, over which, atheist though he be, he prays and weeps.

I can see theologians of a certain stripe, a somewhat self-satisfied stripe, pouncing on this, pounding the pulpit, pronouncing with every assurance, with too much assurance, "Gotcha." Derrida has walked right into their clutches, confirming what Augustine has been saying all along. Whenever we desire something, anything, no matter how transient the satisfaction it gives, what we really desire is the everlasting satisfaction that only God can give, even if we do not know that it is God. Radical theologians, deprived of a pulpit, would respond to this, not with a counterpunch, but with a question. What is to say that the opposite is not the case? Why not conclude that those who say they love God have found words to do service for their love in and under the name of "God," but that this name is one of many names for something-I-know-not-what?

As the philosophers say, God is the unconditional, but the unconditional is not God (Lesson Two). No one has been granted privileged access to the unconditional, an inside track on what the mystics call the "cloud of unknowing," the unknown God, the *Deus absconditus*. These unnerving masters of nonknowing, situated in the very heart of religion, who have regularly riled the powers that be in religion, freely admit that, when we come up against the limits, when we reach the borders of knowing and nonknowing, we are trading in symbols, dealing in imaginative figures that issue from the depths of our imagination. What is being confessed in all confessions, from

Augustine to Derrida, is our nonknowing, the mystery widely known as "God."

Is what we love and desire *really God*? Or is "God" a stand-in for what we *really love* and desire? When we say, "God is love," is "love" our best name for God, or is "God" our best name for love? This is a conflict reason cannot settle. There is an undecidability here beyond our reach to resolve, but it is unreachable in a positive way because the undecidability protects us from doing injury to the event. If we knew what we love is *really God*—or anything else, for that matter, like someone saying it is really the way our DNA programs us—that would prevent the event. The event would evaporate under the intense heat of that identification. What is going on in the name of God would collapse *into* the name of God; the unconditional would be contracted into the conditional; the undeconstructible would be walled inside a construction. Love would come equipped with the power and prestige of God, with the intimidating majesty of God. Then we would know exactly what we had to do, would have it on the highest authority, and we would, to that extent, know what we are doing, in the nominative, having thereby attenuated our responsibility in the accusative. The secret would be out. The something I know not what would be reduced to what I know.

But the inquiry into the event must do it no injury. It must carefully cultivate the mystery that, despite all we do know—and the more the better—in the end, we do *not really know* what is going on in any final or decisive way. Situated in the middle, between the unprethinkable facticity of the beginning and the unforeseeability of the end, we are forever *inquietum*, quietly, disquietingly, quite exquisitely, ecstatically *open*. That passion of nonknowing drives what Derrida calls "religion without religion," a "doublet" for religion found outside religion. This religion "repeats" religion but this time without the doctrines and the rites of religion in the strict or confessional sense of the word but not without the event, its heart for the event, its restless heart. Radical theology is the repetition of classical theology, without the assurances the latter affords.

How far is this from Tillich, when he says that religion is a matter of placing our unconditional faith and love in something, with or without religion in the narrow sense? What remains of the distinction between theology and philosophy once we have rendered the distinction between the religious and the secular porous? Once we start talking about the love of what is going on in the name (of) "God," boundaries become permeable.

I can also see theologians of a certain stripe, an increasingly frustrated stripe, saying, "Enough! Let's be honest." The difference between Augustine and Derrida is that Augustine *really* believes in God and is *seriously* seeking to know the God he believes in, whereas Derrida's religion is a clever riff, a slippery send-up, a dexterous ruse, a postmodern Parisian parody, and his confession the literary conceit of an *atheist* (used as term of abuse). From this, theologians of a more radical stripe would calmly beg to differ. The difference is, rather, that Augustine has a community and a stable vocabulary with which to express his love, supplied him by his Christian-Neoplatonic tradition—of which Derrida is deprived, deserted, desertified, decertified. Derrida, in a quasi-Jewish and slightly atheistic voice, is praying and weeping in the dark, writing a memoir of the blind, using borrowed names, knowing that he does not know the name of what he loves or if his prayers are any more than postcards lost in the mail, errant messages bobbing in a bottle. But these obstacles do not obstruct his prayer; they incite it (Lesson Four). They do not prove him irresponsible; they intensify his responsibility. He has no eternal support, no external authority to back him up or answer his prayers. He is left *coram deo*, meaning *coram* something-I-know-not-what, something going on in the name of the God whose name he learned in his mother's arms.

One reason I find Augustine's question so rich and suggestive is that it *assumes* love, assumes *that* we love, assumes that we are beings of love and hope and desire, and so the only thing in question is *what* we love. Unless we are insipid, saltless, soulless and "mediocre fellows" (Kierkegaard), we all end up loving something, like it or not, and the real question is axiological, whether what we love is *worthy*—worthy of us, worthy of our love, worthy of *what is going on in the name (of)* "God," and whether we are making ourselves worthy of what is happening to us.

Jacked up a notch in academic jargon, which could make an impression at happy hour, I am saying the *unconditional* is not finally and precisely a matter of unconditional *being* but of being's unconditional *worth*. The unconditional does not refer to what *exists* unconditionally (the ontological), because at present we are being told nothing does; it refers to what is *loved* unconditionally (the axiological), what we cherish *for itself.* Our calling is to be unconditionally loyal to the unconditional, to make ourselves worthy of it. Even if, *especially* if, ontology ends in a ruinology, love holds its ground. Even if, especially if, death finally reigns throughout the universe, life is worth living worthily. The glory of life emerges, not *after* death, which is the mystification, the supernaturalization, the literalization of the figure of the resurrection, but *in* the face of death—that is, over and against the inescapable horizon of mortality. The star of the axiological rises in the dying of the ontological light.

■ ■ ■

Love Is Without Why. The sole task that remains now before we call it a wrap and take our bows, *s'il y en a*, is finding how to go about determining *what* is worthy of our love. For that we again call upon the resources of the mystical tradition. We should never trust anything that has not passed through the filter, the screen, the discipline, the criticism, the confession, the circumfession, the crucifixion—in short, the radicalization of mystical nonknowing. This nonknowing is nothing negative; it is a positive passion. It is creative, not destructive. It does not leave us in despair but it sustains our hope and drives the search. It is not apathy but the aching of our restless hearts, a passion impelling us forward into the future, into something-I-know-not-what, until death pulls us apart. This nonknowing does not breed the indifference of skepticism; it ignites the passion of our love—of the future, of the to-come, of the promise/threat, of the coming of what we cannot see coming. Derrida quips that here ontology becomes "hauntology": the Spirit becomes a specter, the *Geist* a ghost, a call of unknown provenance.

So, then, what aid do the mystics offer? Love, the Rhineland mystics say, is "without why." We love because we love, and there is no answer as to why we love because there is no question. Johann Scheffler (1624–1677), the mystical poet who used the pen name Angelus Silesius, packed a great deal of wisdom into a very short couplet:

> The rose is without why. It blossoms because it blossoms;
> It cares not for itself, asks not if it is seen.

Love is like the rose. The blossoming of the rose is *how* we love. Love releases the axiological realm by releasing life from its servitude to some other, servile purpose. Of course, we would all love to have our love returned with love, but that is not a condition of love. That is its risk, down on bended knee, heart pounding, hoping for a yes, yes. Love is transformational, not transactional. When we love we do not start by calculating what is in it for us or demand to know what purpose it serves. Faced with the unprethinkability of being and the unforeseeability of the future, love does not ask, "Why?" Love's only question, the one true question, the question of all questions is, "Is it unconditionally worthy of affirmation, in itself, for itself, without why?" What is truly loved is loved simply for being there rather than not. We love what is intrinsically worthy of our love, prized and appreciated *for itself*, not for its use value or its exchange value, for enjoyment (*frui*), not employment (*uti*, use), Augustine said. We love the thing itself, not something else we can get back in return. It is treasured for itself, not because it is a good investment, which is how Derrida distinguished a "gift" from an "economy." Love is precious because it is aneconomic, priceless, an expenditure not dependent upon a return.

Sapientia, the Latin word for *wisdom*, comes from *sapere*, savoring, to taste, as in having a palate for a fine wine; savoring is something more than quenching our thirst or washing the food down. In axiology, the love of wisdom (philosophy) is the wisdom of love. Love is distinguished from foolishness; loving wisely, unconditionally, worthily is distinguished from loving unwisely, with something up our sleeve, unworthily. The psalmist says it is the *fool* who says in his heart that there is no God, not the stupid person or the atheist or the secular humanist! Foolishness is not a failure of intelligence but a failure of the *heart*. If you can smile and smile and be a villain, you could also be a fool and have a high IQ. When we love unwisely we turn love against itself; we turn ourselves against ourselves; we turn God against God. Foolishness is not a cerebral but a cardiological condition, a dislocated heart, having your heart in the wrong place, or a sclerotic heart, a hard heart that needs to be softened. Foolishness lies in the pursuit of what is *unworthy* of us. The ship of fools carries several passengers on board, but they all diminish themselves by demeaning the end into the means, foolishly subordinating the unconditional to the conditional: the good to accumulating wealth, truth to acquiring power, ethics to rules, faith to creedal correctness, art to fashion, honor to fame, friendship to gaining influence. The list is long, unlovely, and well known. Like the poor, it is always with us.

■ ■ ■

The Real Atheism. Fiery preachers love to castigate "soulless atheism," which I have to admit does carry a rhetorical punch. Who wants to be soulless? So, perhaps they will be consoled to learn that even in radical theology there is an *atheism*—there is more than one atheism, just as there is more than one theism—that can be used as a term of abuse, an atheism that really is *unworthy* of us, a truly toxic atheism, a "Lord, what fools theses mortals be" foolishness. This atheism is found not in rejecting the existence of an entity called God but in rejecting the *event* that is going on in the name (of) "God." In this sense, the Godless are indeed soulless villains, loveless louts, barefaced hypocrites, empty shells, the whited sepulchers Jesus criticized, no depth, no faith, no love, no heart, no shame, no salt. In the scriptures, salt is an axiological not a mineralogical category; it is the criterion of truth.

When Jacques Derrida says he "rightly passes for an atheist," it is the "rightly passes" that warrants our attention. This means that Derrida *correctly* checks off the "atheist" box on the census form, which is making an inventory of positions not affirmations, of propositions not events, of creedal beliefs not faith. But when Derrida *also* says ("circumfesses") that he has been asking himself Augustine's question all his life, he reveals what the census conceals. The census records what is propositionally "correct," but it passes right over the heart of the *truth*, the truth of the *heart*. Derrida does not embrace any creedal "belief" (*croyance*), neither theistic nor panentheistic, but he is not without *faith* (*foi*), which has to do with the event, what is in his heart.

Here, in a nutshell, is what I am going for:

The name (of) "God" is not the name of an unconditionally Supreme Being up there (theology).

It is not the name of an unconditional ground of being down here (ontotheology), although that is getting warm.

It is the name of what we affirm unconditionally, of what we *love*, without reservations, without qualifications, *without why*, which is that in which we really believe (axiology).

Radical theology is a meditation upon matters of genuine worth, a search for what we really can believe, a matter of making ourselves worthy of what is happening to us. If you get that, you got your money's worth from these lessons.

What we love may have many names, but whatever name it assumes it names something for which we are willing to put ourselves (*not others*, please note) in harm's way. The call of the event is a call to action. The name of God, Kierkegaard says, is a deed, a *work* of love, a life of prayer, which is not a matter of beads and candles, of incense and dimly lit churches. It is not a question of taking monastic vows—been there, tried that—but of vowing ourselves unconditionally loyal to something of unconditional worth. That is why Bonhoeffer called for a "new monasticism," in the world, the one that to our great surprise they told us we "left" back in the novitiate. This is what gradually made Thomas Merton, the famous monk, more and more uneasy with monastic life. It is what the Catholic theologian Yves Congar called a new *laïcité* (secularity), which weakened the distinction between the religious and the secular. The religious vow may be kept in an artist's studio or a scientific laboratory, in an Ebola clinic in a dusty west African village or a courtroom defending people who are too poor to defend themselves, in underequipped hospitals and schools in the worst neighborhoods in the city, in efforts to save the trees or to protect endangered species, in the humble works and days of everyday life, shopping for a new hat.

■ ■ ■

The New Revised (Not So) Standard Version of Matthew 25. One of my favorite examples of loving without why is found in Matthew 25. Lord, when did we see you hungry and give you to eat, thirsty and something to drink? If you did this to one of the least of mine, the Lord answers, you did it to me. There is the axiological point. The righteous undertook these works of mercy *without knowing* that these were the Lord's own. The nonknowing, the secret, was crucial:

> Why feed the hungry? Because.
> Why bother? It is without why.

The hungry were hungry, and the sick were sick, and the imprisoned were imprisoned. Period. Enough said. That is the pure gift, an expenditure without the *expectation* of a return. Gratitude may or may not be forthcoming, but that was not the point. The pure gift is given no matter what, without condition. The righteous were responding to the *call* that rises up in *axiological glory* from bodies laid *ontologically low*, from humble, hungry, thirsty, imprisoned bodies, to which they responded *unconditionally*, without reserve, *without why*.

This story narrates the event going on in the name (of) "God" perfectly. That is how the event happens, how the kingdom comes, one by one, in singular acts of selfless service, which "cares not for itself, asks not if it is seen." The kingdom comes *by* the gift, *by* the unconditional, *by* the impossible. The kingdom comes true, not as a great eschatological world-historical transformation but micrologically, locally, intermittently, episodically, obscurely. The kingdom comes every time the hungry are fed, whenever the naked are clothed, whenever and wherever the little ones, the least among us, the nothings and the nobodies (1 Cor. 1:28), are lifted up, whenever the last are made first.

That is the kingdom. Tout court. End of story.

Alas, that is not the end of the story. Its author—an economist (a tax collector)—walks the whole thing back. He frames it within a larger Economy of Salvation, where a fearsome Son of Man comes to separate the sheep from the goats, reimbursing the righteous for their expenditures with eternal treasures and making the not-so-righteous pay up in the coin of eternal fire. Thus do the works of mercy mutate into the works of mercenaries. The kingdom of God is not supposed to be the *reward* for the works of mercy; the kingdom of God *is* the works of mercy, what the world would look like when the event going on in the name of God holds sway, where every trace of an economy of reward and punishment has been sent packing, economics being a dismal science.

So here would be still another opportunity for a timely rein-carnation. If I could come back as a medieval copyist assigned to copy Matthew 25, I would lose that part, or maybe add a line that by eternal fire Matthew meant putting a torch to your life in time (which I doubt). I would be willing to put up with the monastery cold and the lack of indoor plumbing in order to save this text from itself. The explicit telling of the story annuls its very point. Once we have *read* this story, the *secret is out*. We cannot unring this bell. Now the righteous *know*. Love me and I will reward you beyond all imagination. Love me not and you will rue the day you were born. Can you imagine the stunned look on the faces in the congregation if the bride and groom made marriage vows like that? They would empty the place. The celebrant would walk off the altar. The caterers would quit. Nobody would attend the reception. That is not love. That is a threat. In the courts, they call it spousal abuse. In radical theology, we say God has fled the scene, leaving us with 𝕲𝖔𝖉, and praying God to rid us of 𝕲𝖔𝖉.

Lesson Twelve

SO WHAT?

TODAY, THANKS to contemporary cosmology, the vast expanse of the universe is spreading out before us. We are being invited to adopt a cosmic perspective, to see that our planet, on which the lives and loves of everyone who has ever lived have taken place, is but a "pale blue dot," "suspended on a sunbeam" (Carl Sagan), in a vast celestial expanse. Today, the glory of love glows amid the gloomy prognostication that, if it holds up, may make physics the ultimate dismal science (Lesson Seven). It is not eternal fire that lay in store for us but the prospect of eternal burnout, planetary overheating, solar exhaustion, star death, cosmic heat death. The "ground of being," which started out as the principle of the everlasting being and power of the world, ends up as a *theopoetic* word of praise, an exclamation of joy over the world, *while it is still here in all its transient glory*, like a shooting star that burns brilliantly for a brief moment and then disappears. The first version of panentheism is a canticle to the everlasting cosmic spirit. The revised version, in which cosmotheology becomes cosmotheopoetics, celebrates the *passing* glory of a world that lasts for the while that it lasts, that blossoms because it blossoms, after which the cosmic spirit gives up the ghost.

■ ■ ■

Once There Was a Spot, Until There Was Not. To go back to the King Arthur legend, planet Earth is like a cosmic Camelot, where once there was a spot, where for one brief shining moment there were gods and humans, oceans and mountains, good and evil, suffering and joy, the whole uncontainable, unclassifiable, unprethinkable panorama we call the world, where the universe, taking note of itself, ratified itself and said yes, *oui, oui*, yes, yes, amen. I entertain no illusions of being a reincarnated Angelus Silesius—or Carl Sagan, for that matter—but allow me to offer, with all due apologies to the society of poets everywhere, dead, living, and to come, a little quatrain about the mystical rose of today:

> Let it never be forgot,
> once there was a spot,
> only a pale blue dot,
> until there was not.

Then the universe moved on, and nothing remained of this little planet and the rather nondescript middling star (astronomically speaking, don't tell the Greeks) that warmed it.

But wait. That is really going too far. That is just flat-out nihilism. That's Macbeth. "Life is a tale told by an idiot, full of sound and fury, signifying nothing." In "The Meaning of Death," a 2005 episode of the long-running (but not endless) BBC hit *Silent Witness* (it's about forensic pathologists), whose title translates its musical theme, a very spooky Latin song called "Testator Silens," a couple of self-styled Nietzscheans undertake a wanton killing spree on the grounds that the universe is ultimately meaningless. That is good TV but bad Nietzsche. The *nihil*, the vanishing, is the *nihilism of grace*. The *not*, the *no*, is the setting of a sweeping doxology of the yes, yes! Not "Out, out, brief candle," but "Burn, burn!—and, please, not too brief!" Life will always have been too brief.

Still, if what is coming is cosmic oblivion, how does that fit with the prayer "Come, yes, yes"? Why pray for that? Where is the future in that? Where is the hope?

That is the right question. I am saying the finitude is intrinsic to the love, that it keeps love safe. How so? In radical theology, which is about *life*, life is hope in life, as long as there is life, as long as its negentropic force can hold up against the forces of entropy. If we give up that hope, life is as good as dead. So to live is to call for more life, as long as we can make it last. "Come" is the anthem of life in the face of death. I never cite the rest of Augustine's *cor inquietum* line, *donec requiescat in te*, until our hearts rests in you, because resting in peace is not my idea of a good time. It is no time, RIP, death, a nihil pure and simple. The finitude keeps the "without why" safe, allowing love to love *without an expectation of a return*, which keeps the future open—until it is *not*. The glory of love does not come as an eternal reward for love. It is embedded *in* the love, intensified by its transiency. *Sic transit gloria mundi. Sic transit gloria dei.* Love's call is unconditional. "Come" is a call that calls come what may.

As Plato said, when we run up against conceptual limits, against the very border dividing knowing and nonknowing, we need to make do with the next best thing, which is to tell good stories, likely stories. For all his complaints about the poets, Plato was quite a poetic soul himself. He was the author of a famous allegory of the human condition as living in a firelit cave where we have daily commerce only with shadowy copies of reality. Then along comes a philosopher who emancipates us by leading us to the light of the upper world, where we see the real things themselves. There we behold the source of the life and growth of all things, that in which we live and move and have our being, *the sun*—the blinding, brilliant, glorious Greek one!—whose everlasting light and inexhaustible heat is a sensible symbol of supersensible being and eternal truth, world without end, amen! Had Plato been Irish, he might have come up with a different version of his allegory, but if you have ever been to Greece and seen that sun, and the brilliant white stone buildings that reflect it in all its glory, you will understand that the great man could be forgiven for mistaking both the symbol and what it is the symbol of! If not, when you do go there, indulge yourself in the Platonic illusion.

Today we are told that when we look up at the vast heavenly vault of stars at night, as I did as a child, it could be (it's not likely) that we are seeing the light that has just reached us from a star that is actually dead, which, who knows, may once have been the sun of a flourishing world like ours, of which we know nothing at all. Were that so, should we say now that their life then was in vain? Are we to conclude that there was no sense, no truth, no beauty, no worth, no value in such a world because it did not last forever?

So I propose an alternative allegory, an updated post-Platonic myth. Imagine that that star would (someday) be *our sun*, which would, after an unimaginable amount of time, reach a place at an unimaginable distance, where other (unimaginably other) intelligent beings would look up and see it without realizing all it had left behind—that would be *us*, all the countless and long forgotten generations, all the love and hate, all the cowardice and bravery, nobility and ignobility, cruelty and kindness, by then long dead. Are they to say the same thing then of *us now*? That our lives and loves, our works and days, were all in vain because they did not last forever? Or does the patina of our mortality make these moments all the more precious, like lovers holding fast to each other in the night because they know that in the morning they must part?

But that is a sad story.

So what? It is sad but beautiful, and the sadness is ingredient in the beauty. Unlike the Greeks, who fell in love with the lure of the everlasting, the transiency intensifies the beauty of the moment and deepens the joy. Happiness is upset by sadness, but joy surmounts it and is unshaken by it.

At the end of a great film, as the credits roll down the screen, do you demand your money back because it did not last forever? At the end of a beautiful song, do you applaud, or do you complain that it is over? Is that not the meaning of Sister Death?

So, then, why did the string quartet on the *Titanic* continue to play? They were applauding. They were saying by playing, playing in order to say, yes, alleluia, this is what life has been, a beautiful moment in the cosmic music of the spheres, yes, a shooting star, a flicker of glory, beautiful but brief, beautiful because brief, not everlasting life and everlasting Greek glory, but a more difficult glory, sadly ending but beautifully blending with the sadness.

Yes, yes, amen, alleluia.

Axiology is a doxology.

Glory be to life, which however it was in the beginning, and however it will end, will always have been too brief.

■ ■ ■

So What if Everything Just Vanished? The unconditional is unconditional, and God is God, and what is going on in the name of God holds sway, even if, *especially if,* in a time beyond counting, the whole thing vanishes without a trace, and the world dissolves in entropic dissipation, in eternal oblivion not eternal glory. Just as the sun rises on the good and the bad, and the rain falls on the just and the unjust, so, too, the consuming fires of the cosmos will have consumed all, *the sheep and the goats*— leaving Matthew's celestial accounting books eternally unbalanced. Why, O Lord, do the wicked prosper? Because they can, and they have the means to get away with it. They always have, and my money says they always will.

The unconditional is the powerless power of the call, the response to which does not calculate either its worldly fortunes or even its cosmic outcome. The unconditional is the quiet call of the possible, of the possibility of the impossible, like the one that called John Lewis and his sisters and brothers across the Edmund Pettus bridge in Selma, Alabama, on Bloody Sunday, 1965 (some of whom, I wager, "rightly passed for atheists"), wearing only the breastplate of justice, their loins girt about only with truth, where, as usual, the loins of the law (the Alabama state troopers, the powers and the principalities) were girded with gun belts. The unconditional is unconditional, and God is God, and what is going on in the name (of) "God" holds sway, even if, *especially if,* everything that happened that day, if everything that is written in the stars, including the stars themselves, is destined to be erased.

Fiat Deus, ruat coelum. Let what is going on in the name (of) "God" be done, even if the whole world perishes.

What if everything just vanishes?

So what?

A PARTING WORD (OR TWO)

YES, YES

THE FINAL lesson will be a *lectio brevis*, meaning "mercifully short," less a lesson than a parting word. By the very terms of radical theology there are many words of elementary import, many ways to name the event across many different cultures, times, and places. Then why single out "God" for special attention? Why grant this particular name special privileges? Why does radical theology need to bring up God at all? Strictly speaking, it does not. The name *God* is a placeholder for an absolute secret. It need never come up. It is endlessly and undecidably translatable into other names of elemental import. The unconditional does not care what we call it.

So why did I choose it? Strictly speaking, I did not. It chose me, before I had a chance to say a word. I had very little to do with it. As soon as I awoke in the world, the world was already up and running, and someone not of my choosing stepped in and swore allegiance for me to this name, all of which was transacted for me without my consent. As best I can recall, I was never consulted in the matter. Mind you, I am not complaining. That is as it should be for us ground-diggers. We all begin where we are, in the concrete conditions in which we find ourselves, and start digging for the unconditional. But you can start anywhere. I am here telling my own story on the wager that you can translate it into your own life, that it will serve as a prism in which you will recognize some of yourself. My "god-parents" vowed I would keep the vow they vowed to God on my behalf, and I in turn I have been doing my best. Were I ever visited in my dreams by them and asked if I have kept this vow—"Do you still believe in God?"—I would tell them that I have undertaken to be loyal to this name, to the *event* that is going on in this name, to be unconditionally loyal to the unconditional, in which we live and move and have our being, which is both radically unprethinkable and radically unforeseeable.

So serious was I that I supplemented this vow with religious vows of poverty, chastity, and obedience. These were "supererogatory," over and above the call of duty, "counsels of perfection," all in the name of rising above earthly conditions in order to live an unconditional life, where we prayed, "Let us remember that we are in the holy presence of God," repeating that prayer every hour. While I gave up my canonical vows—there is such a thing as too much perfection!—I never gave up my religious vocation, my calling (*vocare*), my response to the call that is going on in the name (of) "God," what I am calling the mystical sense of life (Lesson Five). I never gave up this life of prayer, never stopped praying "Come," never stopped trying to observe this rule, albeit with a little tweak, a little supplement. This, I admit, would have raised the suspicions of my superiors back in the day, that the name (of) "God" is not the name of an assured presence but of a tremulous coming-to-presence, of a soft voice that disturbs the peace of the present and pries it open to the prospect of what is coming. Now I pray, "Let us remember that we are in the presenc*ing* of God, of the coming to be of God, of the insistence of God, of the may-being of God. Let us remember that we are summoned to be part of the history of God, of God becoming God in the world. Let us remember that with *God*, with the *event* that is harbored in the name (of) "God," all things are possible, up to and including *the* impossible."

Once a week, back in the novitiate, we would make what was called in our *Rule* a *reddition*, a French word meaning to give an account of ourselves, a spiritual rendering, in a consultation with the master of novices. This man was a veritable maestro of the ascetic life, who knew all the highways and the dead ends, all the ins and outs, all the consolations and desolations of living a life of prayer. I think of this little book as my imaginary report to my spiritual director of old. I cannot imagine, I can only imagine, what effect reading it would have had on this good man. He lived to be a hundred years old, and we were sure he survived by the sheer force of a disciplined will. Talk about Nietzsche's "ascetic priest!" Had he lived long enough to read this confession, this circumfession, of the spectral condition of my spirit, I am sure he would have promised to pray for me, for someone so much in need of prayer. If he asked me whether I still pray, I would say, "Like mad," knowing full well that he would consider what I mean a little mad. But I would assure him that I do pray, now more than ever, from out of the depths, abyss to abyss, hoping against hope, *veni, Sancte Spiritus,* come, *viens, oui, oui,* yes, yes, I said yes, alleluia, world without why, amen.

FURTHER READING

LESSON ONE

Like every good introduction, I intend to lure you into further reading. There is no improving on John A. T. Robinson, *Honest to God* (Philadelphia: Westminster, 1963) for a lucid, engaging, now-classic introduction to the posttheistic scene of theology in the twentieth century. *The Palgrave Handbook of Radical Theology*, edited by Christopher D. Rodkey and Jordan E. Miller (Cham: Palgrave Macmillan, 2018), is an excellent way to get up to date on radical theology. I also recommend the work of Robin Meyers, who is both a pastor and a professor, especially *Saving Jesus from the Church: How to Stop Worshiping Christ and Start Following Jesus* (New York: HarperCollins, 2010); and *Saving God from Religion: A Minister's Search for Faith in a Skeptical Age* (New York: Convergent, 2020). I spell out more carefully what I mean by radical theology in *In Search of Radical Theology: Expositions, Explorations, Exhortations* (New York: Fordham University Press, 2020), especially in the introduction. I mention Jacques Derrida a lot. He is difficult to read but he was never clearer than in a Villanova University Roundtable with him, which I published along with an extended commentary, entitled *Deconstruction in a Nutshell: A Conversation with Jacques Derrida*, edited with a new introduction (New York: Fordham University Press, 1997, 2020). Here you will find a discussion of everything in Derrida to which I refer, including secondary sources, and, if you have the courage to read him, Derrida himself.

LESSON TWO

Like Bishop Robinson and countless others, I have been deeply influenced by Paul Tillich, whose name also appears throughout this book, three of whose works are not to be missed. Paul Tillich, *Theology of Culture*, edited by Robert C. Kimball (Oxford: Oxford University Press, 1959) (here I quote page 25); *The Courage to Be* (New Haven, Conn.: Yale University Press, 1952), especially pages 182–90; and *Dynamics of Faith* (New York: HarperOne, 1957). His rediscovery by a generation of younger theologians can be found in *Retrieving the Radical Tillich*, edited by Russell Re Manning (New York: Palgrave Macmillan, 2015). I also repeatedly refer to St. Augustine's *Confessions*, especially books 1 and 10. Of the many good translations, I prefer Frank Sheed's (London: T and T Clark, 1944). I cut my theological teeth on Frank Sheed's *Theology and Sanity* (New York: Sheed and Ward, 1947). F. W. J. Schelling, Tillich's muse, is also a challenge to read, but my reading of him, along with references to reliable secondary literature, can be found in my *Specters of God: An Anatomy of the Apophatic Imagination* (Bloomington: Indiana University Press, 2022), chapters 4–8. *Specters of God*, chapter 1, contains a more detailed explanation of theopoetics.

LESSON THREE

Mary-Jane Rubenstein's work on "pan(icked) theology" and pantheism is nicely condensed in "The Matter with Pantheism," in *Entangled Worlds: Religion, Science, and the New Materialism*, edited by Catherine Keller and Mary-Jane Rubenstein (New York: Fordham University Press, 2017), 159–66. I cite here Paul Tillich, *A History of Christian Thought: From Its Judaic and Hellenistic Origins to Existentialism*, edited by Carl E. Braaten (New York: Simon and Schuster, 1967, 1968), 391, 265.

LESSON FOUR

I elaborate the prayer of a radical theologian in "Do Radical Theologians Pray? A Spirituality of the Event," *Religions* 12:679, https://doi.org/10.3390/rel12090679 (accessed December 21, 2022). In "Circumfession: Fifty-Nine Periods and Periphrases," in *Jacques Derrida*, edited by Geoffrey Bennington and Jacques Derrida (Chicago: University of Chicago Press, 1993), 154–55, Derrida explains that he "rightly passes for an atheist." I make use of Jean-Louis

Chrétien, "The Wounded Word: Phenomenology of Prayer," in Dominique Janicaud, Jean-François Courtine, Jean-Louis Chrétien, Jean-Luc Marion, Michel Henry, and Paul Ricoeur, *Phenomenology and the "Theological Turn": The French Debate* (New York: Fordham University Press, 2001), 147–75. Elizabeth Johnson's *She Who Is* (New York: Crossroad, 1992) is one of the best ways I know to get over patriarchy, theological and otherwise. I also strongly recommend *The Face of the Deep: A Theology of Becoming* (New York: Routledge, 2003) by Catherine Keller, in my view the preeminent process theologian in the Anglophone world.

LESSON FIVE

I am discussing *Hegel's Lectures on the Philosophy of Religion: One Volume Edition: The Lectures of 1827*, edited and translated by Peter C. Hodgson (Berkeley: University of California Press, 1988), which are as clear as Hegel gets, which for nonspecialists may mean as clear as mud. I get into the tall grass on Hegel and Schelling and try to clear things up in *Specters of God*, chapters 3–8. For the life of Tillich, see Wilhelm and Marion Pauck, *Paul Tillich: His Life and Thought, Vol. I, Life* (London: Collins, 1977), 40–56. Arne Unhjem, *Dynamics of Doubt: A Preface to Tillich* (Philadelphia: Fortress, 1966) is an excellent and overlooked introduction. Coleridge refers to "the willing suspension of disbelief for the moment, which constitutes poetic faith" in chapter 14 of his *Biographia Literaria* (1817). See *Samuel Taylor Coleridge: The Major Works*, edited by H. J. Jackson (Oxford: Oxford University Press, 2009), 314. The *nouvelle théologie* of the Jesuit theologian Henri de Lubac incurred the wrath of the Vatican for its critique of supernaturalism; see his *The Mystery of the Supernatural*, translated by Rosemary Sheed (New York: Crossroad, 1998).

LESSON SIX

If you want to see how to start with Yeshua of Nazareth and end up with the Council of Nicaea, my favorite account is Geza Vermes, *Christian Beginnings: From Nazareth to Nicaea* (New Haven, Conn.: Yale University Press, 2013). For an engaging presentation of the historical Jesus by a contemporary master, see John Dominic Crossan, *Jesus: A Revolutionary Biography* (San Francisco: HarperCollins, 1995), which I call his "baby Jesus book," meaning there is a bigger, more technical one. For more on heaven on earth, see N. T. Wright, *Surprised by Hope* (New York: HarperOne, 2008). On the 1960s "death of God" movement, see Thomas J. Altizer and William Hamilton, *Radical Theology and the Death of God* (Indianapolis: Bobbs-Merrill, 1966), which the authors dedicated to Tillich. The reference to C. S. Lewis is to *Mere Christianity* (London: Collins, 1952), 54–56 (book 2, chapter 3). For a compact, lucid account of how David Strauss proposed an alternative to the dichotomy between naturalism and supernaturalism inspired by Hegel, see Marcus Borg, "David Friedrich Strauss: Miracle and Myth," *Fourth R* 4, no. 3 (May–June 1991), https://www.westarinstitute.org/editorials/david-friedrich-strauss (accessed December 21, 2022). I analyze Schelling's critique of Hegel in *Specters of God*, chapters 7–8.

LESSON SEVEN

Philip Plait, *Death from the Skies* (New York: Penguin, 2008) is an engaging presentation of the scientific account of how the world could end. For a philosophical reflection on this point, see Jean-François Lyotard, *The Inhuman*, translated by Geoffrey Bennington and Rachel Bowlby (Stanford, Calif.: Stanford University Press, 1991), 8–23. For a theological reflection, see John Polkinghorne and Michael Welker, eds., *The End of the World and the Ends of God* (Harrisburg, Penn.: Trinity, 2002). If you are pulling for endless universes, see Paul J. Steinhardt and Neil Turok, *Endless Universe: Beyond the Big Bang–Rewriting Cosmic History* (New York: Broadway, 2007); and Mary-Jane Rubenstein, *Worlds Without End: The Many Lives of the Multiverse* (New York: Columbia University Press, 2014). My view is in *Specters of God*, chapters 13–15; and *Cross and Cosmos: An Anatomy of the Apophatic Imagination* (Bloomington: Indiana University Press, 2018), chapters 11–16. On theology and posthumanism, see Jennifer Thweatt-Bates, *Cyborg Selves: A Theological Anthropology of the Posthuman* (London: Routledge, 2012); and Ilia Delio, OSF, *Re-Enchanting the Earth: Why AI Needs Religion* (Maryknoll, N.Y.: Orbis, 2020).

LESSON EIGHT

In *Deconstruction in a Nutshell*, chapter 5, I elaborate the event in terms of the "call" of justice in Derrida; also, check the index entries "come" and "future." If your local adult evening school offers a course on Martin Heidegger, *Being and*

Time, translated by John Macquarrie and Edward Robinson (New York: Harper and Row, 1962), do sign up.

LESSON NINE

On how Derrida addresses God and religion, see *Deconstruction in a Nutshell*, chapter 6, and the index entry "impossible"; see also his "Circumfession." I spell out these matters in *The Prayers and Tears of Jacques Derrida: Religion Without Religion* (Bloomington: Indiana University Press, 1997). I also highly recommend Steven Shakespeare, *Derrida and Theology* (London: T and T Clark, 2009). The God of the possible is variously defended in Richard Kearney, *The God Who May Be* (Bloomington: Indiana University Press, 2001); and Catherine Keller, *The Cloud of the Impossible* (New York: Columbia University Press, 2015). For a detailed argument on behalf of "weak theology" and the "dangerous perhaps," see my *The Weakness of God: A Theology of the Event* (Bloomington: Indiana University Press, 2007) and *The Insistence of God: A Theology of Perhaps* (Bloomington: Indiana University Press, 2014). See also Richard Holloway, *How to Read the Bible* (London: Granta, 2006), 88–89.

LESSON TEN

Schelling first proposed that whether God will have existed remains to be seen but he did this in a metaphysical register, which must be reiterated in an axiological register. I discuss this in *Specters of God*, chapter 6.

LESSON ELEVEN

See Augustine, *Confessions*, book 10, chapters 6–8; and Derrida, "Circumfession," 122–26 ("What do I love?"), 153–57 (religion without religion). I elaborate the Augustine-Derrida comparison in *Prayers and Tears*, 281–329, and my view of axiology in *Cross and Cosmos*, chapters 15–16; and *Specters of God*, chapter 15. Martin Heidegger, *The Principle of Reason*, translated by Reginald Lilly (Bloomington: Indiana University Press, 1991) contains a magisterial rendering of Silesius's "The Rose Is Without Why," which has never left me since I first encountered it writing my doctoral dissertation on Heidegger. See *Angelus Silesius: The Cherubinic Wanderer*, translated by Maria Shrady (Mahwah, N.J.:

Paulist, 1986), 54. The best introduction to Eckhart is Bernard McGinn, *The Mystical Thought of Meister Eckhart: The Man from Whom God Hid Nothing* (New York: Crossroad, 2001).

LESSON TWELVE

Carl Sagan, *Pale Blue Dot: A Vision of the Human Future in Space* (New York: Ballantine, 1994). Visit https://www.youtube.com/watch?v=wupToqz1e2g (accessed December 21, 2022).

INDEX